Can the Tories Lose?

Can the Tories Lose?

The Battle for the Marginals

edited by
Gareth Smyth

Lawrence & Wishart
London

Lawrence & Wishart Limited
144a Old South Lambeth Road
London SW8 1XX

This edition first published May 1991

© Lawrence & Wishart, 1991

Each essay © the author, 1991

Research and Profiles © Common Voice, 1991

Photoset in North Wales by
Derek Doyle & Associates, Mold, Clwyd
Printed and bound in Great Britain by
Dotesios, Trowbridge

Contents

1 Introduction   7

2 The Meaning of Major *David Marquand*   10

3 Marginal Decisions *Tim Johnson*   20
    Key to Categories   30

4 The Parties Set Out Their Stalls   35
Interviews with Charles Kennedy and Austin Mitchell

5 Putting Parliament in Touch With the People   54
Nina Fishman

6 Profiles of the Marginals   64
    London   65
    Midlands   80
    North East   93
    North West   101
    Scotland   116
    South   123
    South West   140
    Wales   150

Index to Profiles   155
Notes on Contributors   157
About Common Voice   159

Contents

1. Introduction

On 22 November 1990 Britain came to a standstill. Margaret Thatcher, Prime Minister since May 1979, announced that she would resign the leadership of the Conservative Party. An era was at an end.

Her successor John Major has adopted a very different style. Gone is the aura of ideological certainty. Gone is the hectoring of other European leaders. Gone is the assumption that 'there is no such thing as society'.

The Labour Party, revitalised in opposition by Neil Kinnock, has seen some of its key policies incorporated by the Government. In a manner recalling Disraeli's 'stealing the Whigs' clothes' in the 1860s, the Conservatives have jettisoned the hated poll tax, threatened the abolition of the Shire counties, and identified the improvement of education and training as the 'Big Idea' for the future.

The set-piece battles of the 1980s – over the sale of Council homes, nationalisation versus privatisation, nuclear defence, and the European Community – are now of historical rather than current interest. Politics has moved on.

The two major British parties reflect a wider public sense that Britain has 'fallen behind' other countries in the European Community. The relative success of Social Democratic Parties in Europe and Scandinavia attracts Labour, and within the Conservative Party there is increasing talk of 'Christian Democracy'.

Yet both parties either fail to understand, or are unwilling to accept, the real implications of such 'Europeanisation'. Portraying itself as in tune with the European mainstream suits Labour's attempts to undermine the credibility of the Conservative Government, but becoming 'Social Democratic' would surely entail a serious examination of centre-left realignment, a commitment to electoral reform, and a more distinct economic policy.

Becoming 'Christian Democratic' for the Conservatives would necessitate not just a weak commitment to 'consultation' over the reform of local government finance, but the abandonment of Thatcherite economics and an acceptance of the legitimate role of both the regions and organised interest groups in governmental decision-making.

With both major parties competing, in however hesitant a way, for the centre ground, the Liberal Democrats have refused to be squeezed. With a more coherent political programme than ever before, and capably led by Paddy Ashdown, the 'dead parrot' secured a stunning victory at the Ribble Valley by-election and has revived in the polls.

Even in a state of flux, some things remain constant. The outcome of the next general election will be determined in less than 150 of the 651 parliamentary constituencies. And while the number of marginal seats has declined steadily in modern times, the extent of regional diversity and local variation has increased. The 'uniform swing' is a thing of the past, and all the parties increasingly target their efforts on the constituencies which really matter.

Can the Tories Lose? explores these fundamentals of the coming general election.

David Marquand examines 'The Meaning of Major', pinpointing the unique and antiquated role of the 'sovereignty of Parliament' in British politics, and showing how it underpinned the two issues that toppled Mrs Thatcher, the poll tax and Britain's relations with the European Community. He examines the direction in which John Major is taking the Conservative Party and assesses his chances of succeeding where Mrs Thatcher ultimately failed.

In 'Marginal Decisions' Tim Johnson lucidly explains the basics of election arithmetic. He illustrates the different thresholds that have to be passed for the Conservatives to lose either their overall majority or their status as the largest party in Parliament, highlighting the 'decider seats' which would be crucial in a 'hung' Parliament. It is in these 'decider seats', he argues, that voters will choose not only their own Member of Parliament but the nature of the next Government.

The opposition parties have had 12 years of Tory rule to develop their alternatives. Austin Mitchell and Charles Kennedy, both with refreshing candour, answer questions on how far Labour and the Liberal Democrats have come, and what their prospects for success may be in the election.

Nina Fishman argues for 'Putting Parliament in Touch with the People', eloquently castigating an electoral system in which only the votes cast in a small number of seats determine who governs the country. Her impassioned plea for fundamental reform of our electoral system is one that seems likely to win more and more converts in the times ahead.

Finally, *Can the Tories Lose?* provides a guide to the crucial battleground, the marginal seats. From Lands End to (nearly) John O'Groats these seats offer a finely woven tapestry of people, events and issues: over a hundred stories have begun, with their conclusions as yet unwritten.

Thanks are due to all who made this book possible: to the Joseph Rowntree Reform Trust who generously funded the research; to the contributors; to prospective candidates, MPs and workers from all parties who patiently co-operated with our enquiries; to journalists the length and breadth of the country who shared their local knowledge; to the members of Common Voice for their encouragement; and to Matt Seaton at Lawrence & Wishart who imposed deadlines with good humour. I should particularly like to record a debt to Robert Waller, not just for his invaluable advice on 'Marginal Decisions', but also for the inspiration of his definitive *Almanac of British Politics*, recently republished in its fourth edition and an irreplaceable tool for all who seek to understand the electoral geography of Britain.

Any book as current as this is vulnerable to the occasional factual error, which I would be more than happy to have pointed out. The views expressed are those of the individual contributors and not necessarily those of Common Voice as a whole.

Gareth Smyth
April 1991

2. The Meaning of Major

DAVID MARQUAND

Like all great events, Mrs Thatcher's fall and John Major's rise were, on one level, accidental. Had she been less outspoken in her contempt for the rest of the European Community, had Geoffrey Howe been less deft in his attack on her, she might have stayed in office. At the same time there was a logic in her fall, and there is also a logic in the changes which Major has made since he succeeded her. It is with these logics that I shall be concerned.

I begin by recalling the issues which caused her to fall. Two came together. One might seem on the surface to be of little long-term significance, though it was extremely important in terms of everyday politics. The other was plainly of great long-term as well as short-term significance.

The first, *apparently* minor, issue was of course the poll tax. There is no doubt that it was the extraordinary unpopularity of the poll tax which led to the extraordinary upsurge in the popularity of the Labour Party in the summer of 1990. There is no doubt either that it was this that led many Conservative MPs to think that they had no chance of winning the next election if Mrs Thatcher stayed in office, and that created a sense of impending doom in the Conservative Party, without which the political crisis which culminated in Mrs Thatcher's fall would not have taken place.

The second, obviously profound, issue was of course Britain's possible participation in some form of European Monetary Union, looming behind which was the broader question of Britain's relations with the rest of the European Community. By the time Mrs Thatcher fell, the Government was deeply divided on the question of our relations with the Community. Mrs Thatcher was almost certainly in a fairly small minority in her own cabinet, and a number of powerful cabinet ministers had come to the conclusion that they could no longer tolerate her negativism, her shrill and almost hysterical negativism, on the question. Geoffrey Howe's speech in the House of Commons was the fuse which fired the rocket which caused the crisis, and it was Europe that led him to fire it.

There are obvious differences between the question of the poll tax and the question of our relations with the rest of the European Community, but both are bound together by a common thread. They both have to do with the structure, the assumptions and what might be called the legitimising myths of the British state. Both become painful questions, divisive questions, questions which aroused passions strong enough to lead Conservative MPs and a Conservative cabinet, against all the normal and well-known pressures of the system, to rebel against a sitting Prime Minister, because both of them, in different ways, were related to a deep-seated and long-standing crisis of the British state.

I see the crisis in the following way. Thanks to its traditional structure, its traditional assumptions and its traditional myths, the British state cannot handle satisfactorily the set of questions posed by the rapid integration of the member states of the European Community necessitated by the Single European Act of 1985 (which, ironically enough, Mrs Thatcher agreed to, even though it became fairly clear soon afterwards that she had not understood its full implications). The first dimension of the crisis, in other words, has to do with the upwards transfer of authority, competence and power from the national level to a supra-national level – a necessary consequence of the process of integration in Western Europe which began in the 1950s and which has speeded up in all sorts of important ways over the last few years.

The British state is uniquely incapable of dealing with the questions which arise from the upward transfer of competence and authority from the national to the supra-national level. The reason is that at its very heart lies the doctrine of absolute and inalienable parliamentary sovereignty: the doctrine that the Crown-in-Parliament is in some absolutely fundamental sense the possessor of a little hard ball of sovereignty, which it cannot give up, or even share with other levels of government, without ceasing to be the Crown-in-Parliament. The notion of shared sovereignty, which is common in federal systems like the German Federal Republic and the United States of America, is deeply alien to us, because it cuts across this central notion of the absolute sovereignty of the

Crown-in-Parliament. The result is that when we are faced with the need to make significant upward transfers of competence and authority from the national to the supra-national level, we find our state balks. It does not know how to react; it cannot handle the problem.

Not only is the British state uniquely ill-fitted to cope with the upward transfer of competence and power, it also seems to be incapable of divising a stable pattern of relationships between the national level and sub-national authorities. The poll tax, it is important to remember, was only the last of a long series of agonising policy changes which started to be introduced almost from the very moment the Conservatives came to power in 1979, all of them relating to what the centre saw as an illegitimate and outrageous challenge from local authorities to its rightful power. How, ministers asked themselves, can we allow locally elected authorities in Liverpool, Manchester, Edinburgh or Bradford, to decide how to spend the money they have collected from their own ratepayers if they are going to do so in a way which conflicts with the economic priorities of the central state? The central state could not tolerate uppity behaviour of this sort, so a whole series of measures were devised to stop local authorities from engaging in it. The poll tax was only the latest of these. It was designed to make local authorities which spent too much money unpopular with their electors by forcing the increase onto the shoulders least able to bear them. It backfired badly: the Government was blamed, not the local authorities. But the purpose of the whole exercise was to curb the freedom of local government, and it seems clear that the Government's alternative to the poll tax will curb it even more.

Both of these problems, or sets of problems, have been evident in our politics for a very long time, long before Mrs Thatcher came to power, and that point needs to be grasped if we are to understand the dynamics of the Thatcher regime and its collapse. As everybody knows, Thatcherism was about the free economy. But, as Andrew Gamble has pointed out, it was not only about the free economy, but also about the strong state. Both halves of that phrase are equally revealing and equally central to the phenomenon of Thatcherism. I shall not say much about the free economy aspect of Thatcherism, though I shall refer to it in a moment. I wish to concentrate on the other half of Gamble's phrase, on the strong state. I see Thatcherism as a rearguard action, undertaken to restore the authority of the British state, and I believe that that rearguard action was the core of the project.

Why was it necessary? Why did anybody think the authority of the state needed restoring? Why did those who thought so believe they had to change course in a rather dramatic manner to achieve their purposes? The reason, I believe, is that, by the late 1970s, three different challenges had called the authority of the state into question. The first was the challenge of nationalism north of the border and, to a lesser extent, west of the Severn. The second was the challenge of European integration. The third was the challenge of producer-group power.

To most English people, the first challenge was incomprehensible, irrational, even absurd. The English have never really understood that the United Kingdom is a multi-national state. They think of the words British and English as interchangeable. But to people north of the border and west of the Severn, to the non-English nations of this multi-nation state, the fact that it *is* a multi-national state has always been very familiar and very important. When the Scottish Nationalists suddenly appeared on the scene in the 1960s and 1970s, in the process threatening the Labour Party's survival as a potential party of government, the gap between the English and non-English understandings of what it is to be British suddenly became obvious.

The result was a chapter of muddle, self-deception and confusion of purpose. The political class did not know what to do. They could not deal with the Scottish question in the obvious way – by instituting some form of federalism within the United Kingdom. That would have been the rational solution, but federalism or quasi-federalism was ruled out because it risked destroying the whole notion of absolute parliamentary sovereignty. Absolute parliamentary sovereignty is, by definition, incompatible with federalism, which is about shared or divided sovereignty. And so the London Government brought forward a series of mutually inconsistent legislative proposals in which no one really believed and which were patently designed to buy off trouble. The result was the fall of the Government, and its defeat at the subsequent general election.

That, however, was only the beginning of the story. The issue of the territorial constitution of the British state, the issue as to how power should be separated by area within this multi-national state, did not go away. It went underground for a while, but was then reborn. In the last general election, parties committed to Home Rule for Scotland won an absolutely overwhelming majority of Scottish seats. Few observers doubt that the majority won by pro-devolution parties will be even larger in the next general election, even if the Conservatives win a majority in the United Kingdom as a whole. The last ten years, in fact, have seen a widening gap between the political preferences north of the border and political preferences in the south of England. So far from disappearing, the question of what should be the relationship between the territorial entities of which the British state is composed and the state itself has become more pressing than it was fifteen years ago. What Mrs Thatcher did was to try and suppress it, or at least to suppress its symptoms. She did this by centralising government ever more ruthlessly. Whenever her governments faced a difficulty in their relations with local authorities, their response was always an *ad hoc* change which gave the centre even more power than it had before. But centralisation only made the underlying problem worse. The territorial constitution of Great Britain is now more fragile than at any time since the Act of Union.

The second great challenge of the 1970s, the challenge of European integration, manifested itself in a variety of ways. The first, and most obvious, is that both major parties were deeply split. The Labour Party was almost torn apart, and although the Conservative split was never as open as the Labour one, it too went very deep. To take only one example, there is no question that one of reasons why Edward Heath was toppled from the leadership of the Conservative Party in 1975 was that its anti-European members had not forgiven him for dragooning them into the division lobbies to vote in favour of the legislation to enact our membership of the Community in 1972-3.

And of course this same issue led to the referendum – the first ever nationwide referendum in the history of this country. The notion of absolute parliamentary sovereignty is logically incompatible with the notion of popular sovereignty which a referendum implies.

On the European issue, as on the central-local issue, Mrs Thatcher tried to put matters on ice. She did not reopen the matter of our membership of the Community – that would have been very foolish politically, as most of the Conservative Party were in favour of membership. But at the same time she behaved, though we were in, as if we were not. She behaved as if the other Community countries were led by a parcel of rogues out to screw the last penny from Britain, and that her job as the representative of the British people (as a kind of feminine John Bull rampant) was to fight her Community partners every inch of the way, on virtually every issue that arose. Looked at from the point of view of domestic politics, it was a very successful operation. She kept the pro-European majority of the Conservative Party on board because she did not reject Community membership outright, and she kept the anti-European minority enthusiastically cheering because she used her famous handbag to belabour all the other heads of government in the Community – a brilliant example of having one's cake and eating it.

The real significance of her policy, however, lies elsewhere. Thatcher Governments refused to face the implications of this issue for the British state. Instead they put it on hold, on the back burner. Their policy was to stay where they were; to disguise a fundamental *immobilism* with the rhetoric of southern English nationalism.

The third critical challenge to the state had to do with the economy. Broadly speaking, it became clear in the 1970s, perhaps even in the 1960s, that a Keynesian-style mixed economy could not be maintained unless the state established quasi-corporatist relationships with the major organised producer groups. The Macmillan and Wilson Governments of the 1960s tried to do this in a rather nervous sort of way. The Heath Government of the 1970s made a much more determined effort to establish a systematic form of neo-corporatism, and was followed in this by the Wilson-Callaghan Government of 1974-9. And the point about this experience is that it was a disastrous failure. The attempt to establish quasi-corporatist relations between producer groups and government did not work. It did not work because the British state, shaped as it was by the doctrine of absolute parliamentary sovereignty, did not know how to establish these kinds of relationships, relationships which depend by their very nature on the sharing of power and negotiation of differences.

The Thatcher Right's alternative was to give up the Keynesian mixed economy, to go back to the free market, to disentangle the state from relationships which would cause it to lose its monopoly of economic policy-making. And the reason that alternative prevailed is that the political class as a whole – the civil service, the quality press and even leading figures in the Labour Party as well as the Conservative Party – could not dispute the premises on which it was based.

The experience of the 1970s, in short, showed that, in a very fundamental way, the British state could not adapt to the technological and economic changes that were transforming the economies of Europe in the late twentieth century. The Thatcherite solution to this problem of maladaptation was to suppress the crisis that resulted, or at least to suppress its symptoms. The real significance of her fall is that it showed this effort, despite having been made by one of the most brilliant and charismatic leaders of twentieth-century British history, could not succeed. Not even Mrs Thatcher, with all her astonishing nose for public opinion, and her amazing ability to canalise public moods into the direction that she favoured, could keep the crisis of the state on ice for ever. In the end, it got the better of her, through the two routes of European Monetary Union on the one hand, and of the poll tax on the other. And that is where John Major enters the story. The question is, what are the prospects for him?

Clearly his political style is completely different from Mrs Thatcher's. In place of confrontation, there is a new consensus, or an attempt to behave as if a new consensus were in existence. It is not a Keynesian social-democratic, mixed-economy consensus in the postwar pattern. It is a 'social market' consensus, Christian-Democratic or would-be Christian-Democratic. I interviewed Christopher Patten recently for the journal *Marxism Today*, and spent about an hour talking to him. At the end of the interview, he came out with a passionate, obviously sincere and very revealing eulogy of the German Christian Democrats, not just on the grounds that they had achieved economic success, but also because of the social solidarity they had managed to promote. The contrast with Mrs Thatcher's views – no such thing as society, only individuals and their families; the Germans a bunch of Boche – could hardly be sharper.

The attractions of a social market consensus are very considerable. Poll data strongly suggest that the British people would like to have a social market if they could get it. As Ivor Crewe, the psephologist, put it, the British people are not for Keynes any more, but they are still for Beveridge. They want a welfare state, but they also want a market economy. They would like to have this combination which seems to work so well in other countries, and they don't see why it couldn't work here. The trouble is that nobody has ever offered it to them in a serious way. And because the British people are, in this sense, serious social marketeers, we are beginning to see the political struggles of the 1990s turning into a struggle over management rather than over purpose and direction. The argument is now not about the direction we should take. The two major parties agree about that: we move towards a social market. For although the Labour Party doesn't call it that, that is what it means. The argument is about who can lead us more successfully in the agreed direction; about whether the Conservatives are better managers than the Labour Party, or *vice versa*.

Plainly it is impossible to tell who will win that argument. But against my prejudices, against my wishes and hopes, it seems to me that John Major has considerable advantages. I know that we are in the middle of an economic crisis, and that the government of which Major is the head was responsible, in its previous incarnation, for the politics which helped to produce this crisis. But politics do not work in a straightforward way. If people are to be forced out of their existing voting habits by an economic crisis, it is not enough for them to be aware that a crisis exists. It is also necessary for them to think that the other lot can deal with it more successfully than the lot who are now in power. Otherwise it is not rational to shift. And it seems to me that the lesson of history is that just as the Health Service is a Labour issue, so the economy is somehow a Conservative issue. No matter how badly the Conservatives run the economy, the Labour Party will never be trusted to run it better. Other things being equal, the more people feel they face an economic crisis, the less likely they are to vote Labour. That does not mean, of course, that the Labour Party cannot win. It is, however, a corrective to the easy assumption that recession is necessarily good news for it.

The switch to consensus politics has, moreover, wrong-footed the Labour Party very badly. Labour leaders clearly do not know what to do in this new situation. Under Thatcher, it was easy: all they had to do was say 'Thatcher', and people replied, 'Oh, my God, anyone is better than that horrible woman'. But no one can say that about Major. He is patently not horrible. And by going out of his way to prove that he is not horrible he has made the adversarial style of politics, which the Labour Party had become rather good at by the end of the Thatcher era, look cheap. For all these reasons, it seems to me that we may be seeing a Japanese-style party system developing here. If that happens, Britain will be a democracy in the sense that there are elections every so often, that people have freedom of speech and association, and that they can vote, in principle, how they wish. But, in practice, the ruling party will be virtually irremovable. Battles about public policy, which will certainly take place, will take place within the ruling party, and will be settled through factional victories and defeats inside the ruling party rather than through the alternation of different parties in office. It would of course be absurd to say this is bound to happen. Social scientists should beware of prediction; and I make none. But to put it at its lowest, it would not be astonishing if something of this sort were to happen. From the point of view of being at the head of the pyramid, the omens for Major are surprisingly good.

But that is not the question that matters most. The really important question is whether Majorism can resolve the fundamental, underlying crisis of the British state as Thatcherism could not. Here the omens are more confused. By definition, further attempts to suppress the symptoms without dealing with the causes are unlikely to work. If Majorism is to be more successful than Thatcherism it will have to tackle the three great questions which baffled the governments of the 1970s and which the Thatcher governments tried, in different ways to brush under the carpet – the questions of what the territorial constitution is to be, of how Britain is to adapt to the integration of Western Europe, and of how British governments are to relate to the producer groups that proliferate in all advanced countries. Also by definition, Major and his colleagues will not find this an easy task: had it been easy, the Thatcher governments would not have funked it. But it would be rash to conclude that they are bound to fail. As the last few months have reminded us, the Conservative Party is both a ruthless and radical organisation: much more ruthless, and considerably more radical, than its opponents. It has survived for longer, and prospered more, than any other right-of-centre party in the world; and it has done so because it has been prepared, in more than one crisis, to jettison old intellectual baggage and find new answers to new questions. The party that passed the Second Reform Act, began the first moves towards a managed economy, and liquidated the British colonies in Africa, is perfectly capable of abandoning the inhibitions which prevented the Thatcher governments from resolving the crisis of the state in the 1980s. It is, in short, an illusion to believe that the emergence of a Japanese-style party system, with the Conservatives as the permanent party of government, would make it impossible for the questions I have mentioned to be answered.

That, however, is only the beginning of the story. Crises of this sort can be resolved democratically from the bottom up, or autocratically from the top down. It is not difficult to imagine autocratic – or at least undemocratic – solutions to the British crisis. Britain would join a European Monetary Union, and might even agree to move towards a form of political union, while blocking all attempts to cure the Community's democratic deficit. The crisis of the territorial constitution would be resolved by emasculating what is left of local government; if Scottish nationalism became too strong to resist any longer, the Scots might be given a form of home rule, on the pattern that used to apply in Northern Ireland, in return for drastically reduced representation at Westminster. A strange, bastardised form of corporatism would re-emerge but instead of the old trio of state, organised labour and private-sector capital, there would be a duo consisting of the state and private-sector capital alone. Indeed the outlines of such a solution are already in evidence. The real reason for fearing a Japanese-style system is not that it would prevent any movement at all. It is that it would be only too hospitable to further moves away from democracy. Mrs Thatcher's autocratic tendencies were unmistakable. I am sure that, as a person, John Major has no such tendencies. The facts remain that the logic of Majorism may well turn out to be as autocratic as the logic of Thatcherism, and that one of the prerequisites of a *democratic* solution to the crisis of the British state may be a change of government.

3. Marginal Decisions

TIM JOHNSON

The Key to Power in the Next Election

In this article I shall argue two propositions: first, there is a good chance that the next election will result in a change of government; and second, this prospect will make the battle for certain marginal seats even more vital than usual. I want to show why this is so, to identify the 'decider' seats which will be at the centre of the battle, and to discuss the factors which will determine who wins them.

Opinion polls since the advent of John Major suggest that neither of the major parties has established a clear lead. At the same time real votes cast by real electors at the Ribble Valley by-election confirm a trend in local government by-elections: that the Liberal Democrats, whilst still trailing the level of support enjoyed by the SDP/Liberal Alliance in 1987, are alive and making progress.

The Hill Labour Must Climb

Labour needs something of a landslide if they are to sweep away the Tory party's almost unassailable majority in the present House of Commons and replace it with a majority for themselves. Mrs Thatcher was returned to power in 1987 with a majority of 101 seats over all other parties, and the figure has been barely dented by losing four by-elections since then. In summary, the 32,536,137 votes cast and the 650 MPs elected on 11 June 1987 were shared out as follows:

	Con	Lab	Alliance	Others
Seats	375	229	22	24
Share of votes	42.3%	30.8%	22.6%	4.3%

'Others' in this context include the Scottish and Welsh Nationalists with six seats between them, the 17 Northern Ireland members (13 of them some variety of Ulster Unionist), and the Speaker – originally elected as a

Conservative, but not playing a party role in Parliament.

These figures show in its simplest form the steep hill the Labour Party will have to climb to begin to challenge Tory control of Parliament at the next election. Should the Liberal Democrats, as successors to the Alliance, and the various 'Others' win the same number of seats, the Labour Party will need to take 51 seats from the Tories to deprive them of their overall majority. Labour will need to win a further 23 seats to become the largest party and 23 more to have an overall majority. Thus Labour needs at least 97 net gains, almost a record landslide, to achieve even a narrow overall victory.

Translating from the seats which need to be won to the votes which will be needed to win them provides a slightly more encouraging view for Labour. The 51 seats where Labour came closest to beating the Tories ranged from York, where the majority was a mere 147 votes, or 0.2%, up to Feltham and Heston, where the Tories were 9.1% ahead. In two of them, Stockton South and Colne Valley, Labour will have to come from third place, overtaking the Liberal Democrats, to win the seat. In the language of psephologists, the Tories would lose these seats, and their overall majority in Parliament, if there was a uniform national swing of 4.55% (half of 9.1%) from them to Labour. (The size of the percentage swing Labour needs to win a given seat is half the percentage majority because it is assumed that each vote lost by the Tories becomes an extra vote for Labour.)

This would also be a big swing in historical terms, but it would still leave Labour 2.4% behind the Tories in the total vote. This could be seen as a return to normality; the votes of the two main parties have been within 3.4% of each other at seven out of the 13 elections since the Second World War. On the other hand, it would still leave the Tories by far the largest single party and fairly firmly in power, perhaps with some occasional help from Ulster Unionist MPs.

The pattern of voting in 1987 means that Labour will have to jump a second hurdle as high again to get a total majority for itself. If winning 51 seats requires a 4.6% swing, winning 97 will require nearly 8.5%, bringing seats like High Peak, Blackpool North and Amber Valley into the Labour camp or on the edge of it. At this point, Labour would be a comfortable 5.5% ahead of the Tories in the national vote – a margin almost as big as Harold Wilson achieved in 1966. In other words, although Labour needs a swing of 6.2% to gain as many overall votes as the Conservatives, it needs a larger swing of around 8.5% if it is to win the crucial marginals and secure an overall majority.

To summarise, if we accept that Labour is almost certain to gain ground on the Tories, but unlikely to lead them by more than 5.5% in the popular vote, there are basically two things which can happen at the next election. If the swing from Tory to Labour ranges from 0 to 4.6%, the Tories will be returned to power with a reduced overall majority. If it ranges from 4.6% to 8.5%, at least in the places that matter, then there will be a hung Parliament.

Power Thresholds in a Hung Parliament

The possibility of a hung Parliament makes the marginal constituencies even more important than usual. In a hung Parliament there will not be the usual simple 'winner takes all' situation which is produced by the combination of our electoral system with the almost slavish submission of our MPs to party discipline. In a hung Parliament there will be a much more subtle shifting in the balance and reality of power, depending on exactly how seats are distributed.

Consider, for example, the simplest model, where the Third Parties – Liberal Democrats, Scottish and Welsh Nationalists – hold their ground except that Labour picks up the three seats held by Dr Owen and his two SDP colleagues in the present Parliament. Allow also for special factors, such as the role of the Speaker, and the fact that there will be one more seat in the next Parliament because booming Milton Keynes is being split into two constituencies. Then there will be a series of thresholds:

Labour wins 51 Tory seats, bringing it to 283	Tories have 325 seats, just losing their overall majority, but still retaining effective control.
Labour wins 60 Tory seats to have 292 total	Tories on 315; probably still the government, but with effective power significantly curtailed.

Labour wins 65 Tory seats, to have 297

Labour could form a government (6% swing) with positive support from 'third parties' (Liberal Democrats/Nationalists).

Labour wins 73 Tory seats, bringing it to 305

Labour the largest party, but Kinnock will still depend on Liberal Democrat support to stay in power.

Labour wins 94 Tory seats, giving it 326

Only at this point will Labour have an overall majority.

The picture gets more complicated if the role of third parties is taken into account as well. Every net gain which the third parties make from the Tories lowers the threshold which Labour needs to reach to replace the Tories in government – while also, potentially, increasing Labour's dependence on the third parties to maintain that government.

For example, if the Liberal Democrats and the Scottish Nationalists were able to take 12 seats off the Tories, Labour would need to gain only 53 seats from them to be on the edge of forming a Government. This would be theoretically possible with a mere 4.5% swing from the Tories to the leading challenger in each marginal. Equally if the task for Labour is not to be even more difficult, the third parties must not have any net loss of seats to the Tories.

Focus on the Marginals

On the basis of the analysis above, the marginal seats can be grouped into five categories: Labour's easier wins, Labour's decider seats, three way marginals, Liberal Democrat targets and Scottish Nationalist targets. These are presented as lists A, B, C, D and E in the table following this chapter.

On each list, the figures show the percentage vote for each party, with figures for what were in 1987 either SDP or Liberal candidates in the Alliance column. Figures for Nationalists include either Welsh or Scottish Nationalists; the Other column includes Greens and all other candidates. The party which was second to the Tories in these seats in the 1987 election is shown in the 'Leader' column. The 'Con lead' column shows the percentage gap between the Conservatives and the party which came second. The last column shows where the constituency is located, by eight main regions.

List A: Labour's Easier Wins

Labour must win most of these seats to reach the threshold of power. They are all seats where Labour came second last time, and they are listed in order of the Tory percentage majority. In the unlikely event that Labour won all these seats but no others – real life swings are much less tidy than that – the Tories would still have an overall majority, so in that sense these are seats the Tories could afford to lose.

List B: Labour's Decider Seats

These are the seats where the election will really be decided; Labour must win many of them to take power. Again, they are listed in order of the Tory majority. The first 46 listed are simply the ones where Labour came closest to the Tories; the last two are special cases. Milton Keynes South West is the new seat carved out of Milton Keynes, where Labour should have a good chance, but the voting figure shown is for Milton Keynes as a whole in 1987. Staffordshire Mid is the scene of Labour's remarkable by-election victory in the Spring of 1990; with a sitting MP Labour will have an outside chance of hanging on to it at the general election, despite the huge Tory majority in 1987.

If Labour wins only a few of these 'decider seats', there will still be a Tory Government after the election; if it wins them all then it will have an overall majority.

List C: Three Way Marginals

There are just nine Tory seats where Labour came behind the Alliance in 1987, but not far behind, plus one special case, Monmouth. With Labour stronger than in 1987, and the Liberal Democrats still short of the Alliance's former strength, there is a good chance that Labour will be able to leapfrog the Alliance vote in some or all of these seats next time, and either beat the Tory or become the clear challenger to them. Labour is very unlikely to gain power without winning some of these seats, but these are the places where the fight between Labour and the Liberal Democrats will be at its bitterest.

Just such a bitter fight seems inevitable at Monmouth, where a by-election is pending at the time of writing. Although Labour came second in 1987, it is not clear they will be able to stay as the main challenger to the Tories in the by-election. If, as seems likely, the Tories lose ground, regardless of who is the main beneficiary, this is a seat where the Tories are likely to be vulnerable at the general election.

List D: Liberal Democrat Targets

These are the seats where the Tories are being closely challenged by the Liberal Democrats, without a significant intervention by Labour. To win any of them the Liberal Democrats will have to offset the relative decline in the Alliance vote since 1987 by focusing efforts and attention on the places where they have the best chance. Any gains the Liberal Democrats do manage to make among these seats could be very significant in a hung Parliament. Like List C, this list does include some special cases; Milton Keynes North East, where the Lib Dems are strong; Eastbourne, where they won the by-election that helped to start the avalanche which removed Mrs Thatcher from power; and Ribble Valley, which tolled the death knoll for the poll tax.

List E: Scottish Nationalist Targets

Just the same as List D, but for the Scottish Nationalists (the Welsh Nationalists are a long way short of winning any additional seats).

This presentation, with seats neatly sorted into separate lists, helps to focus attention on the different issues involved with each broad group. But in real life there will be wide variations between what actually happens in seats which may be listed very close together here. In 1987 there was a modest overall Tory to Labour swing of 1.7%, but it ranged from over 10% in some Liverpool constituencies to over 8% in the other direction in one or two London ones. The degree of variation in swing between different seats seems to be getting bigger over the years, so the range may be even greater in the next election. And even if there is a big swing to Labour in the country as a whole, but the swing is less in the decider seats, then the Tories could still hang on to power against the tide – something they have been good at in the past.

Deciding Factors

So it is not the overall national swing which will decide the election so much as the actual swing in each of these decider seats. In a handful of seats the major factor may be very specifically related to local conditions – a major scandal, a split in one of the local parties perhaps leading to a splinter candidate, an unusually energetic campaign by a challenger. But in many cases the variation between different seats can be attributed to more predictable factors, affecting whole groups of seats in essentially the same way.

Robert Waller identifies the major influences clearly in his *Almanac of British Politics*.[1] They include regional differences, 'incumbency' effects, and tactical voting.

Regional differences tend to reflect the social background and economic experience of different parts of the country and different kinds of community. Contrasting examples which Waller picks out are the 'Pennine textile marginals' and the London marginals. Each group includes about 20 decider seats, quite enough to make all the difference between success and failure, but while Waller sees Labour doing better than its national average in the Pennines, he believes it faces a potential disaster in London. The early 1980s image of Labour as a hard-left party still survives in London, and may be strong enough to offset the effects of recession, mortgage rates, falling house prices and transport crisis on public willingness to support the Tories. Other regional effects that Waller expects, driven mostly by long-term economic change and the differing severity of the immediate recession, include greater Labour success in the North and on Merseyside, and possibly Southern England, offset by relative Tory success in the Midlands, London and the possible beginnings of a recovery in Scotland.

Regional swings at the last election ranged from 5.8% from Tory to Labour in Scotland to a marginal gain for the Tories in the South. Suppose Labour did get a swing of 8.5% nationwide, but 5.8% less in London; Mr Kinnock would be 16 seats short of the overall majority he could otherwise expect.

Incumbency effects are of a very different kind. The statisticians have demonstrated that sitting MPs – incumbents – do build up a personal vote, for themselves as individuals, rather than for their parties. Sadly for those who would like to believe that people matter more than party labels, the personal vote is fairly small, maybe 2% on average (although it is probably much bigger for a few particularly charismatic individuals). If a sitting MP loses despite this incumbency advantage, then next time his or her party not only has to make up for whatever that personal vote was worth, but also needs to overcome whatever personal vote the new incumbent has built up. Thus there is a 'double incumbency effect' of about 2% on average, against the challenger recovering the seat at the following election.

Six seats Labour needs to win next time were seats it lost to the Tories in 1987 – Wolverhampton North East, Thurrock, Ipswich, Battersea, Walthamstow and Fulham. In theory Labour will need, on average, a swing 2% bigger than would otherwise be expected to win all of them back. In practice this effect may not make that much difference on its own. The double incumbency seats are all, except for Fulham, highly marginal so if Labour is going to come anywhere near winning power, it should be polling strongly enough to sweep aside the double incumbency barrier. And in other seats, where the incumbent MP is retiring, it should be slightly easier for Labour to win.

The Role of Tactical Voting

The third special factor which can contribute to the varying swing between different seats is tactical voting. Tactical voting is one of those things which, like the *bourgeois gentilhomme* speaking prose, almost everyone does without thinking about it. Simply put, it means placing your vote where it has the best chance of being effective, rather than automatically voting for the candidate you personally would most like to win.

For tactical voting to work in a first-past-the-post election, voters have to know – or have a very good idea of – which two candidates are going to lead the poll in their constituency. Then they have to be willing to switch their votes from their most favoured candidate to the leading candidate which they would most like to win. This requires being fully aware both of the local political situation and of the importance of the choice they will be making.

There is good technical evidence that tactical voting does indeed happen, and on a big enough scale to make all the difference in a close election. For the 1987 election, John Curtice and Michael Steed showed that many Labour voters switched their votes to the Alliance where they could clearly see their own candidate had little chance of winning.[2]

The size of this effect varied considerably across Britain. In the North and West it was big enough to add an extra 5% to the Alliance vote in constituencies where the Alliance had been well ahead of Labour, compared with what happened where the Alliance and Labour were closer. In the South and East, on the other hand, it made only about a 1% difference.

Curtice and Steed found much weaker benefit to Labour in the reverse situation, where the vote of third-place Alliance candidates was being squeezed. Faced with the need to choose, almost as many Alliance voters switched their vote to the Tory as to Labour. But Curtice and Steed did conclude that, after taking other effects into account, Labour candidates gained some net benefit from tactical voting by Alliance supporters where Labour was the main challenger to the Tories.

1987 probably saw more tactical voting than any previous general election, and the evidence since then is that the general public is becoming still more aware of the possibilities. It is, of course, the very essence of the classic 'Government disaster' by-election. Eastbourne showed it at work, more because the Labour vote failed to rise to meet its opinion poll performance than in its fall from an already low level. In the Ribble Valley by-election an opinion poll showing Labour trailing in third place was crucial to the success of the Liberal Democrats.

There is more widespread, if less spectacular, evidence in the local by-elections which take place every week around the country. These show striking variations from place to place. Often Labour is winning, with the Liberal Democrats relegated to a poor third, or even worse. But where the Liberal Democrats already have a credible base, they continue to challenge and beat the Tories, often with Labour trailing.

Apparently, ordinary non-Tory voters are becoming increasingly willing to concentrate their support on whichever non-Tory party is strongest in a given area – rather than dividing it on the party lines shown in the national opinion polls. The implications for the decider seats could be very significant.

The greater concentration of the anti-Tory vote should help the Liberal Democrats to retain their strength where they were already the strongest challenger in 1987. More than that, they may be able to squeeze the Labour vote further.

Suppose, for example, that in the South and East the Liberal Democrats do as well from the tactical vote as they did in the North and West in 1987, and gain an extra 4% on average. Other things being equal, that alone would win them five of their decider seats: Portsmouth South, Bath, Cambridgeshire North East, Hereford, Richmond & Barnes.

In effect, tactical voting, or more concentrated voting, means that the Liberal Democrats can win more seats while getting a lower percentage of the poll overall. This is exactly what happened in the North and Scotland in the 1987 election; these were the only regions where the Alliance made gains in the election (three seats); at the same time the average swing against the Alliance was higher in these regions than in the rest of the country.

Labour's ability to gain from tactical voting is more problematic, but suppose it did gain an extra 1% on average; this should give Labour at least five extra decider seats.

A ten seat difference in majority will be neither here nor there if Neil Kinnock or John Major are clear winners in the election. But if the outcome is anywhere in the hung Parliament range, ten seats will have a major effect, both on who forms a government, and what policies they are able to follow.

Tactical voting in the seats which would be on the margin if Labour or the Tories ended up with a big majority would make very little difference, except to the individual candidates and their supporters. Tactical voting in the decider seats could decisively change the outcome of the general election.

Voters in the decider seats will be taking the decision for the country as a whole. Many will choose not to vote for candidates with no real chance of winning.

They may switch their vote from Labour to Liberal Democrat in a Liberal Democrat target, because they realise that a Liberal Democrat victory in Richmond, Edinburgh West or Hazel Grove may make a Labour Government more likely. Conversely, of course, nervous Liberal Democrats in places like Pembroke, Calder Valley and Lewisham East may switch their votes to the Tories for fear of Labour getting in; this seems to have been a factor in the 1987 election.

My personal opinion is that on balance this process will favour the challengers rather than the Tory incumbents. But it is quite possible that having looked at the alternatives and become aware of their power the deciders will plump for John Major rather than Neil Kinnock.

At least that will be a sort of democracy. The country will have been able to use its obsolescent electoral system to choose the government it prefers – assuming the deciders are typical of the rest of us. There is no alternative to winning the political argument fair and square if Labour and the third parties are to have a chance at government. The decider seats are where that victory has to be translated into winning the election.

Notes

1. Robert Waller, *The Almanac of British Politics*, fourth edition, Routledge, London 1991.
2. In *The British General Election of 1987*, edited by David Butler and Dennis Kavanagh, Macmillan, Basingstoke, 1988, Appendix 2, pp335-41.

KEY TO CATEGORIES

LIST A: LABOUR'S EASIER WINS
(Seats the Tories can afford to lose)

Constituency	Con	Lab	Allce	Nats	Oths	Leader	Con lead	Region
		Percentage votes in 1987						
1 York	41.6	41.4	14.9		1.0	Lab	0.2	NE
2 Ayr	39.4	39.1	14.8	6.7		Lab	0.3	SC
3 Wolverhampton NE	42.1	41.7	16.2			Lab	0.4	M
4 Dulwich	42.4	42.0	14.5		1.1	Lab	0.4	L
5 Wallasey	42.5	41.9	15.6			Lab	0.6	NW
6 Nottingham E	42.9	42.0	14.7		0.5	Lab	0.9	M
7 Thurrock	42.5	41.0	16.5			Lab	1.5	S
8 Ipswich	44.4	42.6	13.0			Lab	1.8	S
9 Bolton NE	44.4	42.6	13.0			Lab	1.8	NW
10 Battersea	44.2	42.4	11.9		1.4	Lab	1.8	L
11 Stirling	38.3	36.2	14.8	10.7		Lab	2.1	SC
12 Lancashire W	43.7	41.5	14.8			Lab	2.2	NW
13 Batley & Spen	43.4	41.1	14.3		1.2	Lab	2.3	NE
14 Delyn	41.4	39.1	17.0	2.5		Lab	2.3	W
15 Hornsey & Wood Green	43.0	40.0	15.1		2.0	Lab	3.0	L
16 Ellesmere Port & Neston	44.4	41.2	14.1		0.3	Lab	3.2	NW

Constituency	Percentage votes in 1987					Leader Con lead		Region
	Con	Lab	Allce	Nats	Oths			
17 Langbaurgh	41.7	38.4	19.9			Lab	3.3	NE
18 Corby	44.3	40.9	14.8			Lab	3.4	S
19 Nottingham S	45.0	40.8	14.1			Lab	4.2	M
20 Walthamstow	39.0	34.7	25.1		1.1	Lab	4.3	L
21 Tynemouth	43.2	38.8	18.0			Lab	4.4	NE
22 Hyndburn	44.4	39.8	15.2		0.6	Lab	4.6	NW
23 Cardiff Central	37.1	32.3	29.4	1.3		Lab	4.8	W
24 Hampstead & Highgate	42.5	37.6	19.3		0.6	Lab	4.9	L
25 Birmingham Selly Oak	44.2	39.3	15.4		1.2	Lab	4.9	M
26 Warwickshire N	45.1	40.1	14.8			Lab	5.0	M
27 Darlington	46.6	41.6	11.8			Lab	5.0	NE
28 Cannock & Burntwood	44.5	39.5	16.0			Lab	5.0	M
29 Pendle	40.4	35.3	24.3			Lab	5.1	NW
30 Bury S	46.1	40.9	13.1			Lab	5.2	NW
31 Basildon	43.5	38.3	18.2			Lab	5.2	S
32 Streatham	44.9	39.2	15.8			Lab	5.7	L
33 Birmingham Northfield	45.1	39.2	15.6			Lab	5.9	M
34 Birmingham Yardley	42.6	36.6	20.8			Lab	6.0	M
35 Warrington S	42.0	35.9	22.2			Lab	6.1	NW
36 Stockport	41.4	35.3	22.1		1.2	Lab	6.1	NW
37 Coventry SW	43.3	37.0	19.7			Lab	6.3	M
38 Swindon	43.8	36.6	19.6			Lab	7.2	S
39 Barrow & Furness	46.5	39.3	14.2			Lab	7.2	NW
40 Slough	46.9	39.6	13.4			Lab	7.3	S
41 Kingswood	44.9	37.4	17.7			Lab	7.5	SW
42 Sherwood	45.9	38.2	16.0			Lab	7.7	M
43 Westminster N	47.3	39.5	12.1		1.1	Lab	7.8	L
44 Bolton W	44.3	36.1	19.6			Lab	8.2	NW
45 Bristol E	43.6	35.4	20.4		0.6	Lab	8.2	SW
46 Edinburgh Pentlands	38.3	30.0	24.5	7.2		Lab	8.3	SC
47 Lewisham W	46.2	37.9	15.9			Lab	8.3	L
48 Rossendale and Darwen	46.6	38.3	15.1			Lab	8.3	NW
49 Feltham & Heston	46.5	37.4	16.1			Lab	9.1	L
50 Chester	44.9	35.6	19.5			Lab	9.3	NW

LIST B: LABOUR'S DECIDER SEATS
(From a hung Parliament to an overall majority)

Constituency	Percentage votes in 1987					Leader	Con lead	Region
	Con	Lab	Allce	Nats	Oths			
51 Luton S	46.2	36.7	17.1			Lab	9.5	S
52 Elmet	46.9	37.1	16.0			Lab	9.8	NE
53 Pembroke	41.0	31.0	26.1	2.0		Lab	10.9	W
54 Croydon NW	47.0	37.0	16.0			Lab	10.0	L
55 Calder Valley	43.5	33.4	23.1			Lab	10.1	NW
56 Nuneaton	44.9	34.6	19.2		1.3	Lab	10.3	M
57 Harlow	47.2	36.6	16.2			Lab	10.6	S
58 Keighley	45.8	35.0	19.2			Lab	10.8	NE
59 Lewisham E	45.1	34.2	20.7			Lab	10.9	L
60 Ilford S	48.4	37.5	14.1			Lab	10.9	L
61 Derby N	48.9	37.2	13.4		0.5	Lab	11.7	M
62 Dover	46.0	34.1	19.9			Lab	11.9	S
63 Bristol NW	46.6	34.6	18.8			Lab	12.0	SW
64 Vale of Glamorgan	46.8	34.7	16.7	1.8		Lab	12.1	W
65 Southampton Itchen	44.3	32.1	23.6			Lab	12.2	S
66 Southampton Test	45.6	33.3	21.2			Lab	12.3	S
67 Bury N	50.1	37.8	12.1			Lab	12.3	NW
68 Lincoln	46.5	33.7	19.4		0.4	Lab	12.8	M
69 Mitcham & Morden	48.2	35.2	16.6			Lab	13.0	L
70 Chorley	48.0	34.7	16.1		1.2	Lab	13.3	NW
71 Leicestershire NW	47.6	34.3	17.1		1.0	Lab	13.3	M
72 Hayes & Harlington	49.2	35.5	15.3			Lab	13.7	L
73 South Ribble	47.2	33.1	19.7			Lab	14.1	NW
74 Kensington	47.5	33.2	17.2		2.0	Lab	14.3	L
75 Lancaster	46.7	32.4	19.9		1.0	Lab	14.3	NW
76 Putney	50.5	36.1	12.4		1.1	Lab	14.4	L
77 Brentford & Isleworth	47.7	33.2	17.5		1.5	Lab	14.5	L
78 Fulham	51.8	36.7	10.4		1.1	Lab	15.1	L
79 Edmonton	51.2	36.0	12.8			Lab	15.2	L
80 Gravesham	50.1	34.8	15.1			Lab	15.3	S
81 Eltham	47.5	32.0	20.5			Lab	15.5	L
82 Norwich N	45.8	30.2	24.0			Lab	15.6	S
83 Erith & Crayford	45.2	29.5	25.3			Lab	15.7	L
84 Peterborough	49.4	33.6	16.1		0.8	Lab	15.8	S
85 Dudley W	49.8	34.0	16.2			Lab	15.8	M
86 Derbyshire S	49.1	33.2	17.7			Lab	15.9	M
87 Blackpool S	48.0	32.1	19.9			Lab	15.9	NW
88 Davyhulme	46.6	30.4	23.0			Lab	16.2	NW
89 Erewash	48.6	32.1	19.3			Lab	16.5	M

Constituency	Percentage votes in 1987					Leader	Con lead	Region
	Con	Lab	Allce	Nats	Oths			
90 Birmingham Hall Green	44.9	28.2	27.0			Lab	16.7	M
91 Dumfries	41.9	25.2	18.0	14.2	0.8	Lab	16.7	SC
92 High Peak	45.7	28.8	25.6			Lab	16.9	NW
93 Amber Valley	51.4	34.4	14.2			Lab	17.9	M
94 Blackpool N	51.4	34.4	14.2			Lab	17.0	NW
95 Burton	50.7	33.6	15.7			Lab	17.1	M
96 Northampton N	48.0	30.1	20.7		1.2	Lab	17.9	S
97 Milton Keynes SW	47.8	21.8	29.3		1.1	Allce	18.5	S
98 Staffordshire Mid	50.6	24.7	23.2		1.5	Lab	25.9	M

LIST C: THREE WAY MARGINALS

(Where Labour may leapfrog the Liberal Democrats – and Monmouth)

Constituency	Percentage votes in 1987					Leader	Con lead	Region
	Con	Lab	Allce	Nats	Oths			
99 Stockton S	35.0	31.3	33.7			Allce	1.3	NE
100 Cone Valley	36.4	29.1	33.4		1.1	Allce	3.0	NE
101 Conwy	38.7	22.3	31.2	7.8		Allce	7.5	W
102 Plymouth Drake	41.3	24.1	33.3		1.3	Allce	8.0	SW
103 Cambridge	40.0	28.3	30.6		1.1	Allce	9.4	S
104 Stevenage	42.1	25.4	32.5			Allce	9.6	S
105 Littleborough & Saddleworth	43.1	26.0	30.9			Allce	12.2	NW
106 Eastwood	39.5	25.1	27.2	8.2		Allce	12.3	SC
107 Exeter	44.4	22.5	31.8		1.3	Allce	12.6	SW
108 Monmouth	47.5	27.7	24.0	0.8		Lab	19.8	W

LIST D: LIB DEM TARGETS

(Where the Liberal Democrats have the best chance)

Constituency	Percentage votes in 1987					Leader	Con lead	Region
	Con	Lab	Allce	Nats	Oths			
109 Portsmouth S	43.3	13.0	42.9		0.8	Allce	0.4	S
110 Cambridgeshire NE	47.0	8.5	44.5			Allce	2.5	S
111 Edinburgh W	37.4	22.2	34.9	5.6		Allce	2.5	SC

33

can the tories lose?

Constituency	Percentage votes in 1987					Leader	Con lead	Region
	Con	Lab	Allce	Nats	Oths			
112 Bath	45.4	10.6	42.7		1.3	Allce	2.7	SW
113 Hereford	47.5	7.7	44.8			Allce	2.7	M
114 Hazel Grove	45.5	11.8	42.0		0.6	Allce	3.5	NW
115 Richmond & Barnes	47.7	7.1	43.8		1.3	Allce	3.9	L
116 Kincardine and Deeside	40.6	15.9	36.3	6.4	0.6	Allce	4.3	SC
117 Cheltenham	50.2	7.5	42.3			Allce	7.9	S
118 Plymouth Sutton	45.8	16.4	37.8			Allce	8.0	SW
119 Devon N	50.9	6.3	42.8			Allce	8.1	SW
120 Isle of Wight	51.2	5.9	43.0			Allce	8.2	S
121 Oxford W & Abingdon	46.4	14.9	37.4		1.3	Allce	9.0	S
122 Falmouth and Camborne	43.9	20.9	34.6		0.7	Allce	9.3	SW
123 Cornwall N	51.7	6.4	41.9			Allce	9.8	SW
124 Leeds NW	43.5	21.7	33.5		1.3	Allce	10.0	NE
125 Crosby	46.1	17.9	35.9			Allce	10.2	NW
126 Chelmsford	51.9	6.8	40.5		0.7	Allce	11.4	S
127 Pudsey	45.5	20.5	34.0			Allce	11.5	NE
128 Wyre Forest	47.1	18.9	34.0			Allce	13.1	M
129 Twickenham	51.9	8.4	38.3		1.4	Allce	13.6	L
130 Weston-Super-Mare	49.4	11.4	35.6		3.6	Allce	13.8	SW
131 Sheffield Hallam	46.3	20.4	32.5		0.8	Allce	13.8	NE
132 Bristol W	45.5	20.9	31.3		2.2	Allce	14.2	SW
133 Congleton	48.3	17.9	33.8			Allce	14.5	NW
134 St Ives	48.3	17.8	33.8			Allce	14.5	SW
135 Milton Keynes NE	47.8	21.8	29.3		1.1	Allce	18.5	S
136 Eastbourne	59.9	8.8	29.7		1.5	Allce	30.2	S
137 Ribble Valley	60.9	17.7	21.4		1.1	Lab	39.5	NW

LIST E: SCOTTISH NATIONALIST TARGETS

Constituency	Percentage votes in 1987					Leader	Con lead	Region
	Con	Lab	Allce	Nats	Oths			
138 Galloway & Upper Nithsdale	40.4	12.9	14.6	31.5	0.6	ScotNa	8.9	SC
139 Perth & Kinross	39.6	15.9	16.9	27.6		ScotNa	12.0	SC
140 Tayside N	45.4	8.8	12.9	32.9		ScotNa	12.5	SC

4. The Parties Set Out Their Stalls

CHARLES KENNEDY, MP Liberal Democrats

Gareth Smyth: How would you assess the difference that the replacement of Mrs Thatcher by John Major has made to the political scene in Britain?

John Major has taken the sting out of the anti-Tory vote. It had become so personalised, so crystalised on Margaret Thatcher herself, that her very absence is, for many wavering voters, crucial. Mr Major's greatest card was simply that he is not Margaret Thatcher. We are now through the immediate sense of relief people had that she was gone. John Major had a very good war. Now with the poll tax and other domestic issues, we are back to more normal politics, in the way that it hasn't been probably since the days of Wilson and Heath and Callaghan. So basically he's drawn the sting but I'm not sure that he's done a lot more than that just yet.

Has he made significant changes to the direction of the Conservative Party, or is it just a question of style, not hitting other European Heads of State round the head with a handbag for example?

It's certainly style, but it's substance as well. For example, the child benefit pledge in the Budget, abolition of higher rate mortgage tax relief, these are all substantial policy changes which would never have seen the light of day under Margaret Thatcher. I very much agree with Ken Livingstone's view: he hit the nail on the head when he said the No Turning Back Group of Tories are going to realise that they have landed themselves with the most leftwing Tory Prime Minister since Macmillan. His problem at the moment is that he's still got to be one of them until he gets his mandate from the country.

You said that you thought that with the advent of Major, Britain was moving back to normal politics, by which I would take you to mean that the Conservative Party, following Labour, is attempting to

occupy the centre ground. Does that have any important implications for the Liberal Democrats, who would be understood, rightly or wrongly, as already occupying that centre ground?

Let's talk for a minute about what's happening with Labour and the Conservatives. I think it was the late Bob Mackenzie that once said that during the period of Butskellism in the 1950s and 60s, British elections were basically about competing consensus with furious rows about marginal issues. Across a whole range of things, welfare state, mixed economy, there wasn't much to choose and I think we are moving back to that, a kind of a social market consensus.

So, in a sense you should therefore say we must be very frightened because we are going to be squeezed; they are all sleeping in our bed. I think the difference though with the 1950s and 60s, is that there has been the intervening period, the late 1970s and the 80s, which has enabled the third party vote to build up. It's now clearly not going to go away.

Potentially, there is still up to a quarter of the population which wants to cast a vote that isn't for the two main parties, provided there is a viable alternative. They went for the Greens, when we more or less had taken ourselves out of sane politics, during the Euro-elections. But essentially they are there to come home to us.

The Liberal Democrat Policy Document _Shaping Tomorrow, Starting Today_ outlines a policy direction which is _not_ simply about occupying the ground left between the Conservatives and Labour but trying to develop distinctive policies, which perhaps don't fit very easily into a traditional left/right spectrum. How would you sum up the distinctive message of the Liberal Democrats?

Under-pinning everything else – social policy, economic policy, industrial policy – is our basic starting point. Without changing the structure of the system of government – PR and all that follows from that – you are not going to get the right policy mechanism leading to the right decisions. That remains our distinctive pitch.

On top of that, and I don't think these words are taboo, I would sum it up as a social market economy approach. We are not getting back into the ideological debate about who owns what, only in so far as we say that ownership should be more widely spread. Let's have serious competition in the economy and not just public monopolies becoming private monopolies: and more in-built safeguards for the consumer, building up consumers' rights, whether this is a citizens' charter or a patients' charter on the Health Service or whatever. That's our direction, which is, of course, what Mrs Hogg and others are regurgitating through the Policy Unit at number 10 at the moment.

Taking up the point about citizenship, there is a phrase in the policy document – 'unlike the other parties, we shall treat the voters as citizens with shared concerns not as consumers to be coaxed and manipulated'. What does that mean?

If you look at the cycle of electoral politics in Britain, it is very much 'Boom and Bust', the idea being to get the 'Booms' to come just before an election and to get the 'Bust' to come shortly after you have won it. We are saying let's try and get away from that degree of cynicism, which subjugates the economy in the longer term to the short-term electoral cycle.

We want people to think longer-term – now this might be asking the impossible, it's an aspiration. What we are trying to do is stake out a different approach both on electoral politics and on the position that the citizen occupies.

Douglas Hurd is interesting in this respect, he has made many a speech as Home Secretary about 'active citizenship' and there is a lot in that we would go along with. But I think the Conservatives have misunderstood it.

Let me give you an example. The opting-out of schools in Scotland was supposed to bring more parental involvement, a clamp-down on all these 'useless' teachers, and greater efficiency. What's happened – the first thing the new school board decides is that the standard of the whole fabric of the school is totally unacceptable. So they write to their local MP and say 'what's being done about this?', and get on to the Education Department who write back and say we haven't got the resources to do it, so then they start writing to the Scottish Office. Far from turning people into Conservatives by doing this, they have made people more conscious of the failings of their own policy. It's quite amusing, it's coming back on them directly. So, we are for responsible citizenship but I think you have got to recognise it carries a price for government. The Conservatives are seeing it more as an opportunist gambit.

Decentralising power, which is very much a part of what I would understand the idea of citizenship to involve, carries a price. It carries the risk for any government or any authority at whatever

level, that you are decentralising power to people who, if they think for themselves, may disagree with you.

Absolutely, and if you take the thorny subject of local government finance, this is why local Income Tax will never see the light of day under the present regime. When Heseltine said 'nothing's ruled out, nothing's ruled in', I can tell you local Income Tax is ruled out from day one, for the simple reason you will never get HM Treasury to agree variations in the tax rates and therefore, limit the power of the Chancellor of the Exchequer in a macro-economic sense across the country. They are not brought up to believe in that sort of thing.

This was obviously a very important issue in the fall of Margaret Thatcher because the poll tax can be seen not as a one-off, but as the culmination of a series of attempts by the British state to curtail the powers of local authorities. What distinctive message does your party have on the relationship between the central state and local councils or regional authorities?

We are in favour of moving towards unitary local authorities and want a local Income Tax as the basis by which they are financed so that does mean a lot of autonomy. A question was put to Paddy, I think by somebody at Ribble Valley, 'If you had more autonomous local authorities and they had local Income Tax power, presumably you would have to have a capping ability still at Westminster, because the local authority might decide that the local tax was going to be 50% in order to do something crazy'; and Paddy said 'No, no, that would be something fundamentally unacceptable in principle'.

Now I'm not so sure because I think at the end of the day, if you did have something like that happening, you may need some reserve powers for Westminster to step in and say 'wait a minute, this can't happen', but certainly the principle is that you really are handing over responsibility and more financial control to the local community. We are quite serious about saying 'look, you have to live with the consequences of your own decisions, folks'. It's less likely under PR anyway that you will get a hard-left group that want to raise 50% local tax to send bananas to Nelson Mandela, or whatever it is.

So, single tier authorities with a tax-raising power, parliaments within Wales and Scotland and moving towards regional assemblies for England. A more federal UK state.

There are important connections between this and the issue of Europe which was also very instrumental in the downfall of Mrs Thatcher. What is the Liberal Democrat message on the relationship between the British state and the European Community?

Of the three UK party groupings, we have been the most unambiguous about this. Not only are we in Europe but we should be in ever deeper.

This means monetary union, it means really moving towards a single European Community, however you want to term that – effectively a federal Europe. We visualise more power going to the European Community, which means more power to the European Parliament. Mrs Thatcher was always reeling against undemocratic bureaucrats sitting in Brussels throwing up all these directives, but if you want to bring them under some kind of accountability the only way to do it is to do the one thing she wouldn't countenance, to give more power to the Parliament.

You are committed giving the European Parliament equal powers to the Council of Ministers?

Yes, majority voting now, then moves towards some kind of elected basis for the main decisions on a European level. *De facto* it's already happening: if the European Parliament has a debate about draft regulations on vehicle emissions, the chances are the Commission is going to take account. We would make this explicit by giving political power to the Parliament. Power will flow from Westminster to Brussels, and also to Cardiff, Edinburgh and English regions. Westminster would become less powerful in terms of the range of policy it deals with but, hopefully, better at doing what it's left to do.

What is the basis of your argument for an independent European central bank?

First of all, another *de facto* argument. Ever since Nigel Lawson shadowed the Deutschmark, there has been an acknowledgement that the Bundesbank is calling the shots. Either we go on like that, or we have a participating role in a European central bank. But, secondly, in supporting a European central bank, there does now appear to be an assumption within the European Community that you cannot, to use one of Margaret Thatcher's phrases, buck the market politically, and therefore, it is better just in terms of economic principle to have monetary policy reasonably distanced from political control, so that the awful temptation to spend your way out of a problem, or to bust the economy by stoking up for the election, is drastically reduced.

Of course the counter-argument would be that the establishment of an independent central bank removes monetary policy from the control of elected representatives. How would you respond?

To an extent undoubtedly it does. But I can point to the Germans as a good example, and ask the question, over the last 20 years, who has had the more successful economy? The Germans, who have surrendered the right to control their monetary policy to the Bundesbank, or our crowd with the Bank of England and the Treasury? The comparison speaks for itself.

So the bank worked more effectively within broad parameters set by elected representatives rather than through day-to-day supervision?

I think so, yes.

The common link in the two aspects of Margaret Thatcher's crisis, local government and Europe, was the resistance she had to shared sovereignty. There seems to be a peculiar assumption in British politics that sovereignty must at all costs be retained at Westminster. As a Scot you may not share that?

Legally, emotionally, and pyschologically we Scots have a completely different notion. We say that sovereignty resides with the people and that's a feeling that you might get in Yorkshire, but you certainly don't get it at Westminster.

Why is this, because it is very different to, say, the Federal Republic of Germany or the United States of America, or indeed any other advanced country you can think of?

We do still delude ourselves that we are the Mother of Parliaments. When you have gone through generations of families which think that from London you run India, Canada, Australia and half the rest of the globe then I suppose it is going to take generations to move away from believing that you should still run the Highlands of Scotland from London. I think that is changing, slowly.

Secondly, I think the fact that we are an island does make quite a difference. We do not physically feel part of the European continent; people still talk about 'going to Europe' on holiday and we know exactly what they mean. We have psychologically ring-fenced ourselves, but slowly that is eroding. People of our generation don't enter this with the same assumptions as probably our parents did 40 years ago – and we, of course, have not lived through European war.

For all these reasons, there is this protectiveness about the idea of sovereignty and also the illusion that sovereignty is protected by Parliament which, of course, it is not.

All Governments since the Second World War have tended to share this assumption about the vital importance of Westminster sovereignty: both Labour and Conservative have centralised power away from local councils, and integration into Europe has been very half-hearted. Why should the Labour party share what is in origin a Conservative assumption?

The culture of British politics, the education system in Britain, the way in which the political parties have been structured – everything is focused very much on Westminster. If you get yourself elected to Westminster you have 'made it'. If that is what you are brought up to believe, then when you get there, you want to feel you have got as much power as possible – you are not about to start handing it out.

It is changing. A lot of the younger Labour MPs are not just going to be content with 'Socialism is what Labour Governments do'. They don't subscribe to that anymore and they want to see changes in the whole structure.

Paddy Ashdown has spelt out that acceptance of Proportional Representation would be a condition of Liberal Democrat support for any government in a hung Parliament. Given recent developments in the Labour Party – the working party on electoral systems, the decision of the Scottish Labour Party to support electoral reform for a Scottish Assembly – I was surprised to hear Richard Holme say at a recent press briefing that he didn't feel that it was any more likely that one rather than the other of the major parties would accept electoral reform. Is that your view?

I think Richard was probably talking, if you like, parliamentary reality. When you scratch through the surface there is more genuine interest amongst certain sections of the Labour Party than there is within the Tory Party. Labour as a movement is more sympathetic to electoral reform, but once you hit this thing called the Parliamentary Labour Party, it's still a pretty awesome beast on this. Although there are notable exceptions – Jeff Rooker, Robin Cook, whoever – there are many MPs who never appear on TV, whom you never read much about, the foot soldiers, who are against any sort of change and they are the majority.

Can I turn now to the prospects for the Liberal Democrats in the run-up to the general election. You have achieved two spectacular

by-election successes at Eastbourne and Ribble Valley. These have been dismissed by the Conservative and Labour parties as blips: John Major described your party as the dustbin into which protest votes were being poured. What makes you think you can sustain momentum for the general election?

I'm not certain we can, is the first thing I have to acknowledge honestly. But, that said, I did not expect the national polls to give us the lift they have. The lift will be sustained, but I'm not taking it for granted. The local elections will probably be a mixed bunch right across the country but, nonetheless, I think they will probably show us with about a fifth of the votes, the mark of a party in reasonably good health. Also we may have a by-election in Monmouth.

We are going to try to keep in the public eye and try to be seen to be winners where we have an opportunity to win. The minute people think we can win, they will vote for us – and that more than any amount of policy, any amount of packaging, is important. *The Independent* poll at Ribble clearly showed people would shift their vote to us if they thought we could win. It's that more than anything else which will keep up the momentum.

In 1987 the Alliance gained nearly one quarter of the popular vote, and yet you won only 22 seats, because your vote spread out fairly evenly across the country as a whole. In the coming election do you plan to concentrate your efforts rather more finely on seats where you have a real chance of winning?

Yes and no. We certainly intend to concentrate our effort finely in terms of winnable seats. But we are not going to tell people in any consituency, 'please don't vote for us'. We will want as big a national vote as we can get.

If the crude calculation came down to paring down the share of the vote across the country and targetting it a little bit more then, of course, we want seats in here at Westminster. But we are not going to try and be too-clever-by-half about this. There will be particular concentration on certain constituencies, and you well know which ones they will be, but come an election we have just got to lunge for every vote we can get.

Given your stance on PR, you can't be held responsible for the eccentricities of the British electoral system. But suppose a voter in a seat you have no chance of winning comes to you and says, 'I agree with your policies, but why should I waste my vote in this seat?'.

Whether or not a particular constituency is winnable, every vote adds to the overall national share and that is still important. British politics would have been turned upside down in 1983 if we had had more of the popular vote than Labour. If we had morally beaten the Labour Party then, there would have to have been some change to the way that Labour is allowed to be the official opposition with all the perks and advantages of that.

The national share of the vote matters for credibility and for other practical reasons. The most likely way to get PR is to get us elected in larger numbers into the Commons, where eventually we can bargain with others or even eventually be in the position of introducing it ourselves.

However, I would also have to recognise that folk are not daft and they can work things out for themselves. If the voters' objective is to get the Government out, then the Scottish experience last time will ripple into England. In Scotland we gained seats, Labour gained seats, the Nationalists gained seats, quite irrespective really of the standing of those parties in the Scottish opinion polls. In Strathkelvin it was clearly understood that if you wanted to get the Tories out, Labour were the most credible local alternative. In North East Fife or Argyll, it was clearly understood we were the alternative. In Moray it was clearly seen that Margaret Ewing and the SNP were the alternative. Folk can make those judgements for themselves and vote accordingly, and I have no doubt they will do so.

And choose, in certain circumstances, to vote Conservative because they feel that the Conservatives are preferable to Labour?

Yes; obviously less of a fact in Scotland but I think, yes, in parts of England certainly very true.

Active citizens behaving rationally?

Absolutely. These by-elections have now got down to a story of a two-horse race. In Mid Staffs it was Labour challenging the Tory; in Ribble, Eastbourne, it's us. Neath was already a Labour-held seat, but Monmouth will have to come down to this as well. In all these seats at a general election it will be like that too.

Can I turn to another form of squeeze, the media squeeze. In the general election in 1987, and to some extent in 1983, the issues – particularly because of the day-to-day way in which they were worked out, morning press conferences etc – tended to be determined by Labour and the Conservatives. The issues particular to the Liberal Democrats, including Proportional Representation,

tended to be squeezed out. How can you deal with that problem in the forthcoming general election?

We want to hit the ground running fast and early, establishing right at the outset that we are in lively, up-beat mood and very much part of the story. A lot of the campaign has got to be directed at the media first, before the public, getting the media to think in terms of every story having three sides to it. That hopefully will influence the rest of the campaign.

But beyond that, it *is* difficult for us. With Paddy Ashdown we have had the advantage that he came over very well during the Gulf War. He got a massive amount of exposure – the kind of exposure that without a particularly special subject like a war, a third-party leader would not have enjoyed. In a sense he's had a general election campaign level of exposure, so we don't have to go through that process again. People have formed a judgement of Paddy that is pretty favourable – the guy talks sense, he seems to know what he is talking about.

Paddy is a new face, and is now identified. Major is a new face, he's identified too. Kinnock is an old face and he's been round the concert hall before – I think it's going to be difficult for Labour to enjoy quite the sort of razzamataz and sense of euphoria of the last campaign. People have seen the film already. *Back to the Future* may be great, but when you've seen it once, you know the plot.

You first became a Member of Parliament at 23 and you're still not 32, although no doubt in Westminster you are ageing rapidly. What do the Liberal Democrats offer to young people that the other parties don't?

The almost tribal voting loyalties are being eroded in this country. There is more fluidity in voting now and I think that's particularly true of younger people. That kind of voter is bound at least to hesitate in our direction, to have a look at our shop window, whereas perhaps their parents might never have thought of it. Younger voters tend to be concerned about the environment, quality of life issues, slightly longer-term kinds of issues – very much our agenda. We've got a reasonably youngish looking kind of party; one hopes that rings a bell with them. I'm reasonably young, Simon Hughes is reasonably young, Matthew Taylor's young.

A group of young or 'youngish' MP's who are aiming to be around for some time?

God and the electorate willing!

Austin Mitchell, MP Labour

Gareth Smyth: What difference has the replacement of Margaret Thatcher by John Major made to British politics?
A huge one. After 1983 Labour didn't move far enough or fast enough, partly because Neil Kinnock was feeling his way and partly because they didn't realise the scale of the problem. After 1987 the Labour Party began to change and that change was predicated on Margaret Thatcher. We built a lean-to structure up against a colossus – where she was for the market, we were for managing the market; where she had been troublesome in Europe, we were going to be *communautaire*; where she had imposed her will, we were going to conciliate, to consult people.

Indeed, where she had been radical, we were going to be a conservative party. The Tory Party was a party of restless, radical change, which is why they got themselves into a mess – she was pulling things up by the roots, shoving some of it back but throwing a lot away, and in some cases throwing away the roots. With the economy, the professions, television, there was no doubt she was a great radical.

We were the party that was moderate, sensible; that wasn't going to change things if they were working. We were going to change things back where she had made a mess of it, but not very far – we weren't going to re-nationalise everything she had privatised.

It was all predicated on the presence of Mrs Thatcher. As soon as she is gone, the colossus on which we built our lean-to is removed, and the lean-to falls down!
So Major has not just altered the style?
No, it's fundamental. Nobody is going to carry on running down the same dead-end street as Mrs Thatcher, or dig in the same hole. That would be stupid and that's why they got rid of her. He is much the same on economic matters, but on social matters he is much more of a 'wet'. He also listens and consults.

The Labour Party spent four years emptying its skip of all the unsaleable, damaging things, in the hope that it would be filled up by all the discontent Mrs Thatcher was generating. Now the skip has not much in it, and what we have in it has been taken by John Major. Look at the

45

budget: it cut back mortgage interest relief to the standard rate of tax – we were going to do that; he's attacked business rates – we were going to do that; he's attacked offshore funds – we were going to do that; he's increased family allowance, child benefit in line with inflation – we were going to do that. With the local government review, Michael Heseltine prefers unitary authorities – so do we.

The real difference between the parties is how to deal with the economy, which is going to be the Tories' Achilles' heel. But we haven't got entirely convincing alternatives to them. On the Exchange Rate Mechanism, we said we wanted to join, only at a competitive rate; but didn't say anything about that when the Tories joined. We are going to have a higher unemployment rate under a Labour Government, as well as under a Tory Government, if we are going to manage through the ERM.

How on earth do you build a better society without exchange controls, control of interest rates and the budget deficit? Without national economic management we are up the same creek as the Tories with much the same lack of paddle!

What does the Labour Party stand for now. Is it the social market?
Labour's policy review has been implemented by John Major – the electorate's got change without bothering with an election. What is the 'social market'? Nobody knows, it's just a means of saying we will be nicer than the other lot.

Is it a market plus a welfare state?
As it worked out in Germany, it means as much market as possible, as little state as necessary. Basically, a social market means you generate the wealth first and then distribute it.

But doesn't it also mean the involvement of producer groups and private capital in economic management?
It means you want to get the economy growing, and if that's co-operation in management, yes. It's not a new thing. But if it's not set in concrete it will be this much state and that much market.

A return to Butskellism?
Basically. The first part of these terms is always the Tory part. The problem now is what difference would the people get if they elected a Labour Government; that's what people will be asking themselves.

And how would you as a Labour candidate in Grimsby answer that?
The economic policies of John Smith would be very similar to those of

Norman Lamont. I think we would go back to the old 1964 trap of trying to maintain an untenable exchange rate. Any expansionary government has got to devalue the pound.

But under Labour, John Smith, while proclaiming the need to defeat inflation, would attach importance to growth as well. The balance would shift, but it would be a shifted balance, not a stark change. The Tories have now gone back to deflationary economics because it comes more naturally to them. It shouldn't come naturally to us.

Labour has traditionally been regarded as weak on the economy. How can it convince voters that it can manage the economy?

John Smith's perceived level of competence is probably higher than any individual Conservative politician. I don't attach too much weight to that old image of who can handle the economy best. When we were in government, we could handle the economy best. It comes partly from what you know. There used to be a kind of class differential that the Tories were born to rule, from a financial background, better with money than these load of chaps who had never had any – it's not that any longer.

In 1973-4 it was clear that people wanted Labour to come in and clear up the mess. We've always had this role, we wanted to clean up the mess in 1945, again in 1964. So Labour has an image as the modern bucket brigade of the economy. We need to give substance to that image because undoubtedly we shall be coming in, if we do come in, to clear up an enormous mess – a bigger disaster than the Government acknowledges or, I think, than Labour recognises.

Oil gave us a false sense of security in the 1980s which is now being removed in the 1990s. We are back with the old basic problems – unemployment, uncompetitiveness, low productivity, de-industrialisation. The trade balance is the classic indicator that the problem is acute.

Do you think a Labour Government would be drawn in practice towards a more interventionist approach?

Perhaps we would. You have to distinguish between electoral necessity – to prove ourselves respectable, cautious, safe, conservative – and the imperatives of power. You can say at this stage that a Labour Government would be more inclined to borrow, more prepared to increase taxes. These are marginal differences because now the Tories have got to increase taxes and to borrow because of the scale of the recession.

Whether we realise the necessity of devaluation I don't know. Even if we did realise it, it would be silly to say so. I think in pratice we would devalue, and would be driven back willy-nilly to the strategies of the 1970s, simply by the scale of the problem.

How important is regionalism in this?

It is a very good way forward for policies you would traditionally think were socialist. You can be interventionist now on a regional basis and be respectable. We are talking of regional development agencies, regional lending institutions.

And regional government?

It would tie in with regional government. So far Labour's policy is on a voluntary basis because the North would want to, but the South wouldn't know what to do with it. It needs to be everywhere. To plug into Europe, you have to plug in on a regional level because the future will be a Europe of regions cutting out the nation state. Now I don't particularly want to be in Europe at all, but I recognise that if we are there, that's the way it is going and there is no other way of operating.

Where's Labour going on Europe?

We are at the moment the more *communautaire* of the two major parties, perhaps more *communautaire* than the Liberals because, while they are basically Euro-daft, they will also stir up antagonism on the Common Agricultural Policy, which we don't feel it's respectable to do.

Our orientation developed for two reasons – one because the bulk of the leadership are now enthusiastic pro-Europeans. John Smith and Roy Hattersley always have been. Neil Kinnock has become one – he gets on well with other European socialist leaders. Peter Shore's been demoted and moved out, and it has become kind of unrespectable to be anti-European. There's a kind of unenthusiastic majority that tag along with it, and a backwoods group which says 'hang on a minute', but hasn't much alternative to offer.

Secondly, there's been the desire to embarrass Mrs Thatcher, which has made us more pro-European. That's now gone.

So where do we go? I think we probably maintain our present stance. I don't like it but what could jolt us out of it? If we are going to have a successful theme at the next election, it needs to be re-building Britain – in a sense, that's 'anti-European' – but I don't think the Party feels easy with that kind of theme, so they will probably not change the stance.

The other issue that undid Mrs Thatcher was local government …

It was just her hatred of the rates. She wanted to get rid of them and got stuck on the poll tax. So though she didn't like local government – perhaps from something in Grantham, some deep psychological scars there – the real problem was not local government but the rates.

But there has been a trend to centralise powers to the state.

Labour was the party of devolution in the 1980s, and in the 1970s it provided a much higher proportion of spending than the Tories have done, it increased the powers of local government in many respects. Labour has always had its roots in local government and always looked after it.

The interesting thing is the new generation of Tories coming from local government who actually hate it. They want to privatise everything, changing managerial systems and disrupting local government. Labour are much more the party of spreading things around – hence regional government, unitary authorities, and a Quality Commission. If you had a Quality Commission seeing that standards were maintained, this would lead to much better review.

You have been much associated in the Labour Party with the cause of electoral reform. What is the latest on progress?

When we had a policy review, we should have reviewed everything. The committee that's now sitting is really too late to affect the next election manifesto. We shall come to electoral reform eventually. The only way out, it seems to me, is to offer a referendum. If Roy Hattersley came on his knees and said, 'Let's have electoral reform', we'd still have to consult the people. Why not say we'll consult the people. It makes us more electorally attractive, and if we have only got a narrow majority or no majority at all, the Liberals would have to support the Government so they can get electoral reform. It's a strategy which solves all the problems. I can't see an argument against it.

How many current Labour MPs support electoral reform?

I would say perhaps 30 or 40 people. There are a lot of people in a grey area, but you wouldn't expect MPs to support electoral reform because the system elected them. But there is a lot of hedging of bets now. They know it makes sense but they don't want to put their heads above the parapet. If the leadership came out tomorrow and said, 'electoral reform', they would say, 'What a great idea, I was always in favour of it!'.

There is a substantial group of Tories in favour. In the past they were bigger, proportionally, than the Labour group, but we are now probably bigger than them.

But no system which is not proportional will help Labour, the alternative vote won't.

Do you think that if Labour lost again, electoral reform would become a tidal wave?

It would be forced on us, more or less, by the Party or the Unions.

Labour needs a swing of around 8% to win the hundred or so marginals that would give you an overall majority. Is it on?

It means the obstacle between us and power is the greater. The number of marginal seats is less than it was, so any incumbent party is in a stronger position because the tides of change need to rise higher than they did in the past. In our case there is a particular problem in that we didn't do well enough in 1987. We had to get half-way to power in 1987 and we didn't. What should have been done in two steps, now we may have to do in three. All the Tories have to do is avoid losing enough seats.

They could lose 45 and still have an overall majority.

That's a strong position. We are already strong in the North but we have got to make gains in the West Midlands. We've got prospects there, but the real problem is the South, the new towns and London.

What is going to convince the voters there?

Interest rates and unemployment. People were led into thinking they had the secret of the power of credit and the secret of eternal growth. It just wasn't true. It was a confidence trick, and now they are faced with crippling interest rates, no improvement in wages and a threat to jobs. The gilt is off the gingerbread. Everything turns in this election on the scale of recession. The Government's been told by the Treasury there is recovery – that's partly because the Government is obsessed with inflation.

Any idiot can get inflation down. The real problem is how you get pick-up, how you get growth, how you expand the economy when any expansion immediately increases inflation again and widens the balance of payments gap.

How do you?

You can only do it by devaluation. The imperatives are, firstly increasing taxes and borrowing, secondly the devaluation of sterling. If you look at what's happening in the United States, the dollar has come down, exports are doing very well. I watched the *Clothes Show* on television, quite by accident, and it's all American clothes. We might even see American cars coming over, God help us. That's because the dollar is so competitive.

We haven't got that advantage. Interest rates are high, so people are being cautious and saving more, and they've just put VAT up, so consumer demand isn't going to pick up. That's why Jaguar is in trouble and why textiles are in disastrous trouble. Government spending isn't going to increase, so where is the pick-up going to come from? There's now a resurgence of 'confidence', but it's baseless.

Aren't you basically exposing a yawning gap in Labour's economic policies and thus Labour's appeal to these key voters?

I'm not sure of the extent of that. The first lever of change is just reactive – the Government has failed, promised them this but not delivered. I think we are less attractive than we could be.

How much of a problem is the alleged hostility of the national press towards Labour?

It's not important electorally. It's important long-term in changing attitudes and perceptions. In terms of its immediate impact on elections, pretty well nil.

The long-term drip – attacking Neil Kinnock, 'the Labour Party subsidises lunatics', 'throws money about like it's going out of fashion', 'consists mainly of Arthur Scargill and Ken Livingstone waiting behind the scenes', all that kind of rubbish – plus the process of saying the City of London is marvellous, the standing of sterling is all-important – all this is a conditioning process. The *Sun* is appealing to a working-class audience, but there's always been a rough and a respectable working class – there was when I was a kid anyway – and the respectable working class is still the kind that reads the *Mirror*. The fact that the *Sun* has moved from a Labour-supporting newspaper to a Thatcherite paper must have an effect on turning attitudes against Labour, so there's a long-term effect there, but it's not important at any individual elections.

Can I read you something you wrote in 1983 in *The Case for Labour* – 'I joined Labour at Suez time in 1956, everything then seemed straightforward, the Conservative Government was wrong-headed, incompetent and outdated. Britain was a complacent class-ridden nation sadly in need of a backside-booting modernisation to a fair and more equal society'. Has much changed?

No, not really. There is less of a visible elite. While divisions of class are still there, we don't have a ruling class in the sense of a unified class with a lot of little cliques at the top. MPs are not the political elite anymore: we're professional politicians who run the institutions which have failed. So, in a sense, politicians have replaced the class system as the object of popular hatred.

This is now a society of different elites, you in your small corner and me in mine, which don't interact much. The politicians, who used to be the political branch of the upper class, are now just professional politicians trying desperately to keep open a situation which is beyond them.

But it is still an unequal, unfair society and one where the Tory Government has failed more dramatically and more incompetently than any government I've ever seen before. The poll tax was a major piece of absolute incompetence and the way they have robbed the economy is mind-bogglingly stupid. With the Tories of the 1950s it was a mild kind of failure, they just didn't bother, the situation just slowly went downhill. Now they've propelled it downhill out of doctrinaire prejudice. That's the big difference.

Is there going to be a 'backside-booting modernisation'?

The Labour Party is conservative. Our proposals on the constitution aren't good enough but they are a step in the right direction. A diet of change which gives people power, makes people feel better. We need a new kind of plan, a fairly substantial programme of educational expansion and training. In terms of a more equal society we shall tilt the balance, because any government that believes in public spending is going to do that. The heart is certainly in the right place, pulses are moving in the right direction.

We will certainly be better than this lot. Once we've begun on the road, the logic will go further and further, we can't avoid it. As a Party which represents people and can only advance them if it gets going, we shall be forced into policies which will go in the way I want. There's no salvation from the kind of policies we are proposing now, but they will be modified in power.

Do you think Labour has significant policy or political disagreements with the Liberal Democrats?

Their policies are very similar to ours. Their policy on education is exactly the same as ours. And local government is the same apart from local Income Tax and them asking for a federal system. Environment policy is very similar indeed. They are opportunistic on Europe, more genuinely enthusiastic on Europe than we are because they haven't got to drag people like me along with them. So there's all the makings there of a coalition, even the makings of a common platform.

The major obstacle is electoral reform, isn't it?

No, the major obstacle is rigid party thinking, inflexibility. They can't make concessions because it is portrayed as admitting they couldn't win.

Can Labour win?

It's imperative that we win. If the electoral treadmill goes against the Tories, it will become a question of impetus. The electorate would give a further push to the Party it pushed the last time. It is quite possible that we will win on a three-stage process rather than the two-stage process of 1974.

Isn't the alternative, if there were a hung Parliament, some sort of governmental arrangement with the Liberal Democrats?

Well, I hope we would do that. Even that is a triumph.

If Labour did get a majority, isn't that when the problems would start?

No. Labour is very inventive in office. As a process of improvisation the 1974-9 Government was superb. It carried the Unions into an incomes policy which worked, which was effective in reducing inflation without massive unemployment. Investment was good too, throughout that Government, despite the financial and economic difficulties.

The crucial thing is to show that Labour Government works. That is not part of the horizon for many people now. They don't know that Labour is quite good in government and certainly better, for many desirable purposes, than the Tories. To get power, even on a three stage, three election basis allows us to show that it works. That is the crucial thing – not Labour's argument over theoretical policies as in the early 1980s or the argument over public relations in the later 1980s.

There are going to be hard times in the 1990s, the good times are over. And that will in the end bring to power a Party with a sense of purpose and a mission to reconstruct.

5. Putting Parliament in Touch With the People

NINA FISHMAN

Since inscribing my name on the electoral register, I have voted in five general elections. Each time I voted, I felt no compulsion to vote for the Labour Party, even though I have always been a Labour supporter. The strongest feeling which welled up inside me when entering the polling booth was frustration. Because I have always lived in a safe Labour seat, my vote counted for nothing. I might as well have voted for Captain Swing or King Lud.

Like me, the overwhelming majority of voters in England and Wales live in safe seats. Their votes will never have any significance in deciding the outcome of any general election. Nevertheless, like me, about three quarters of them troop out to their polling stations every time. Our collective behaviour is an impressive testimony to the enduring fabric of British political culture. We would feel like shirkers and skivers if we stayed at home. Without ever being taught about voting at school, we know that we have to vote to keep up our end of the democratic compact.

In fact, many people who live in the five hundred odd safe seats do not wonder whether or not their votes actually count towards the result of the contest in their constituency. Most of them actually believe their votes matter; that is what the canvassers on the doorstep tell them; that is what the press and television commentators assume in their reportage. The prevailing assumption of British political culture is that everyone's vote counts because general elections are the pinnacle of our political system. They are the proof shining forth that we live in a parliamentary democracy.

You can easily test for the presence of this assumption yourself. Ask the next group of people in which you find yourself the following question:

'There will be 634 seats contested in Britain at the next general election; how many of them are marginal?' The answers you will get will vary, but within a surprisingly narrow band. Most of us are not psephologists. We remember swingometers if we are old enough, and understand the concept of a marginal seat. But beyond that, most of us neither remember nor care about the minutiae of constituency results between elections.

Your sample will answer the question on the basis of their political culture, which tells them that general elections are the essential proof of our democracy. Therefore, it follows that most of the seats contested *must be marginal*. If they are confident characters, their answer will be that 'most of the seats' are marginal. If they are cautious, they may retreat to '40-50%'. If they are feeling disillusioned and cynical about politics, they may respond cavalierly by saying '30%'.

Almost none of your sample will guess the correct answer, because they have assumed, perfectly reasonably, that if general elections are really democratic, they must also be genuinely risky for politicians. After all, if elections are the time when the people decide, then the people must actually be deciding … mustn't they? On being told that the number of marginal seats is actually between 50 and 100, most of my respondents – mature students on an evening degree course – responded with blank incomprehension and frank disbelief. One person anxiously enquired, 'Should you be saying this in public?' He was worried that I might get into trouble for disclosing information which was, to him, self-evidently subversive.

If the deduction made from a general rule is wrong, then the rule itself must also be inaccurate. Not surprisingly, the revelation that their conclusion is empirically incorrect induces my students to question their general assumption. Your sample will probably respond in the same way. If only a *minority* of seats are really under threat in a general election, how can it be a real democratic contest? The question is logical and ultimately it *is* subversive. It is not surprising that the media are not keen to explain and instruct the voting public in the basic points of psephology. They would immediately incur the determined wrath of both Front Benches. (The BBC, of course, is bound by its Charter to uphold the present system, even when it now comprises mostly rotten boroughs, pocket boroughs and potwallopers.)

The two Front Benches value the legitimacy which a general election confers upon both HM Government and Opposition. Neither have dictatorial designs. Both believe in democracy and in British parliamentary democracy in particular. If the numbers voting in general elections declined substantially, our serious and dedicated political leaders would feel that the fabric of the system was somehow threatened. Similarly, serious pressure would certainly be brought to bear if television news broadcast nightly during a general election campaign, 'Now for the only seats that count. We will look at the campaigns in the Heavy Hundred, where the next government will be decided.'

TV '87, the campaign for tactical voting, experienced exactly this kind of informal, but deadly earnest, pressure emanating from Party headquarters in the 1987 general election. Nevertheless, it is universally acknowledged amongst political scientists that tactical voting is not only a frequent, but also a rational response when the voter is confronted with more than two candidates in serious contention in a first-past-the-post electoral system. The Front Benches, and even the Alliance, found a public campaign for tactical voting an anathema, because it brought another pillar of our political culture into disrepute.

Political leaders readily admit in private that people vote for the party of their second choice to keep another party out. They acknowledge this fact in public only with extreme distaste. Labour tactical voters who voted SLD in the recent Ribble Valley by-election were referred to in the same tone of voice which was reserved for 'homosexuals' 30 years ago and for 'conchies' in World War II. The political establishment's dismissal of tactical voting was echoed by many political commentators. The unspoken but clear message to the rest of us is that whilst tactical voting may occur, it is anti-social, highly regettable and not to be encouraged.

The tone of voice has become increasingly censorious as tactical voting has become more prevalent. Not surprisingly, increasing numbers of voters have responded to the serious three party races in their constituencies by voting tactically. (The Liberal Party's ability to field candidates in more and more constituencies during the 1960s revealed that a bedrock of 10-15% of the British electorate were anxious to vote for a third party alternative. This 10-15% makes all the psephological difference. The electoral arithmetic of first-past-the-post means that their candidacy determines that increasing numbers of MPs are elected on a minority vote.) Since there is no way that the earth will mysteriously open and serious third party contenders will cataclysmically disappear into the hole, tactical voting is also now a continuous part of the political agenda at general elections.

A first-past-the-post electoral system is only 'fair', if a very small minority of votes are given to third, fourth and fifth parties. As soon as more serious candidates than Commander Bill Boakes and Screaming Lord Sutch offer themselves, then tactical voting will attract increasing numbers of pragmatic voters who are keen to maximise the value of their votes, who are interested in their votes actually making a difference to the result. The Fabian Society responded to this situation a century ago by advocating the alternative vote, with voters being able to express a second preference. The Fabians praised the French electoral system, where two ballots were held, because French voters were not forced to waste their votes in order to support the first party of their choice. A century later, tactical voters in Britain are maximising the marginal utility of their votes. Can any Fabian blame them?

It is public knowledge, and well-known to any student of politics, amateur or professional, that people decide how to cast their vote for a wide and interconnecting variety of reasons. Moreover, no erstwhile political scientist has yet succeeded in discovering a social scientific law of voter behaviour to predict election outcomes. Because tactical voting is a rational response to a first-past-the-post contest in which there are three serious contenders, rational people have been doing it more and more frequently over the past 30 years.

Revelations of the small, and ever-decreasing, numbers of marginal seats and confessions of tactical voting are perceived by the political establishment as undermining the political system. Nevertheless, these uncomfortable facts will continue to gain currency in British popular political culture. People in Britain *do* care about elections, and they *do* mind about wasting their votes. In my experience, most people felt that the 1987 Conservative government was a minority government because it had received a clear minority of votes in the general election. Accordingly, they felt entitled to conclude that it lacked democratic legitimacy. There is no doubt that this disaffection contributed to the unease about the introduction of the poll tax.

The political establishment faces three options in dealing with voters' increasing lack of confidence in the electoral system. First, they can do nothing and hope that the third party will disappear as a serious contender. When this happens, the first-past-the-post system will again become fair in the one hundred or so marginal seats. Voters in the other safe seats will still be wasting their time and energy by turning out to the polling booths, but the overall national result can still be described as 'fair'. The problem with this option, of course, is that there is no way that the Liberal Democrats are going to disappear. It is an unrealistic option, which nevertheless appeals to the Front Benches because it involves a minimum expense of time and energy for them.

Second, our political leaders can recognise that the Liberal Democrats will remain an important political force, but still opt to do nothing about the electoral system. They can decide that it matters very little whether voters are increasingly disaffected, even to the point where only 40-50% of them turn out on a general election day. After all, the United States survives as a legitimate democracy with voter turn-outs as low as this. This 'do-nothing' option is cynical in the extreme. Nevertheless, it is the course of action most likely to prevail unless the political establishment is subjected to determined pressure from below. By definition, a vested interest has a vested interest in the *status quo*, and it is not surprising that our Front Benches are keen to preserve their present comfortable positions.

The third option, electoral reform, is the one which is most appealing to voters. It allows us to re-assert our hold over the political establishment. It enables the current fiction of general elections being a serious contest to have a real basis in fact. Electoral reform will give our creaking political system a new dose of vitality and credibility. This option is self-evidently crucial for the continuing health of the body politic. It is not surprising that more and more politicians at Westminster are coming out in its support. Any MP who is clear-eyed enough to observe the growing popular disillusion with politicians knows that electoral reform is the answer.

Electoral reform is not a panacea, but it will enable Westminster to re-establish open and vital channels of communication between Parliament and constituents. At present, most MPs feel so secure that they bother little with what people 'out here' think and feel. We are ignored by those who frequent the corridors of power because the electoral system gives them no reason to heed us. When I explain to students that MPs could always find out what their 60,000 or so voters feel by hiring the local football ground every Sunday morning for a public meeting, they greet my suggestion with derision and disbelief. But they also ruefully acknowledge that their MP has very little incentive to care for their views.

The obvious way to induce MPs to pay more attention to their constituents is to ensure that MPs are more dependent upon their constituents' votes to continue in office. Serious electoral reform will move the goalposts for all 651 MPs. Serious electoral reform will ensure that all 651 MPs feel insecure for at least two generations. It will take them that long to find their way around the new electoral rules. In order to save their seats, they will have to communicate more often and more meaningfully with us out here. None of us expect a weekly voters' meeting. But, we know that we deserve to be taken more seriously by our representatives than we are at present. By giving us votes which mean more, electoral reform will give us additional power over the House of Commons. Is this a bad thing in a democracy?

The political establishment's responsible arguments against electoral reform creak with age. They were first trotted out by the likes of Lord Salisbury, Lord Rosebery and Arthur Balfour in the 1890s. They had real resonance when Britain owned a vast empire, and the British state viewed itself as the centre of the universe. The political establishment then argued that electoral reform would produce weak coalition governments – those strange continental states abounding with fractious and quarrelsome coalitions. Britain had taken a century to evolve the two-party system of government, and it was now the envy of the rest of the civilised world.

Voters, or 'the democracy' as we were described in Victorian and Edwardian political parlance, had their rights. But the British state also had its responsibilities. On balance, the heavy burdens of statecraft outweighed the claims of citizens to electoral fairness. It was the duty of British citizens to recognise this perhaps unpalatable fact and adjust accordingly. In order to preserve world stability and order, British democracy must trim its sails. And, of course, we did.

When Roy Hattersley uses the same argument in 1991, it has a hollow ring. There are no imperial pressures now on the British state to be either centralised or efficient. Few serious cares of state cause the Front Benches worry or present difficult choices. Westminster now has rows and sleepless nights about salmonella in British eggs and our trains' stubborn refusal to run on time. The world is no longer the House of Commons' oyster. Britain can afford the luxury of indulging 'the democracy', and making our votes count. If the state runs less efficiently, it will also run more fairly and we will be consulted more frequently.

In the long term, electoral reform is the most desirable option, not only from the voters' perspective, but also from the politicians'. The disturbing gap between Parliament and the body politic is not going away. It is increasing at a worrying rate. The most far-sighted politicians have realised that the only way to close it is by changing the electoral rules: to force the whole of Westminster back towards the people.

A growing number of prudent reforming MPs want to restore Parliament's tarnished image. As Robin Cook told Charter 88's packed meeting on Bastille Day in July 1990, he felt imbued with a profound regard, and an abiding affection for Parliament, as any MP. I remember his words well because they made a lump come to the back of my throat, 'No MP loves the House more than I do'. His commitment to electoral reform arose from his desire to cleanse the system. He invoked Luther, whose zeal to reform Christianity had arguably saved the Catholic Church from disastrous corruption and the decline which inevitably accompanies decay.

However, electoral reform will not be achieved simply because a growing number of political activists have decided that it is important. Nor will it happen when the Labour Front Bench finally acknowledges its own conversion. Even though growing numbers of concerned citizens agree that electoral reform is an idea 'whose time has come', this expanding consensus of the caring and good is insufficient to prize open the gates of inertia which protect the *status quo*.

As Bernard Shaw noted in his exhortatory leaflet 'Vote! Vote!! Vote!!!' in 1892: 'The right to vote was won for you, not by the great statesmen whose names are connected with the Reform Bills of 1832, 1867, and 1884, but by the persistent agitation of generations of poor political workers who gave up all their spare time and faced loss of employment, imprisonment and sometimes worse in order to get you a share in the government of the country. Now is your chance to use what cost so much to win. The political battle is about to begin. Choose your side according to your conscience; and strike the one blow that the law allows you ... There is no excuse for not voting. Even when there is no candidate worth voting for, there is always some candidate worth voting against.' (Fabian leaflet no.43)

A century later, *votes* are still the only sign whose meaning politicians dare not evade. We have to turn the impending general election into a contest about electoral reform. Fortuitously, we have an excellent opportunity to do so, if we are audacious and determined enough to use it. The advent of John Major has moved the Tories very quickly indeed back towards the centre ground. Under Neil Kinnock's tutelage, the Labour Party has also been propelled towards that same terrain. As a result, there will be less distance between the three parties in this election than there has been for at least a decade. The three manifestos will show only marginal differences on economics, education, the welfare state, defence and even the European Community.

This lack of difference on the 'ordinary' and 'bread and butter' issues means that we can raise the issue of electoral reform and be assured of an interested, even sympathetic audience. People are more alive to the vagaries of the voting system when they are reflecting on how best to cast their own votes. Moreover, as we have observed, the parameters of voting will be throwing up the inequities and ironies of first-past-the-post in a three party race. There will be more tactical voters in this general election than ever before: voters will have moved up the learning curve to the point where they will find the rational calculation of maximising their vote's marginal utility second nature.

British political culture focuses on general elections, and puts voters in mind of not only party differences, but also politics in general. Recent election campaigns have left voters feeling remarkably cold, even hostile. Voters resent being preached and condescended to by politicians whom they accurately perceive as enacting a ritual by which they set remarkably little store. After all, the risks for politicians have been so minimised that general elections present few problems.

Voters' alienation from the general election hustings is symptomatic of Westminster's estrangement from its constituents. But the opportunity remains to capture voters' interest and imagination during a time when it is accepted that everyone thinks and talks politics. If those activists who are lobbying inside the political establishment for electoral reform take it 'outside' during the election campaign, then the electoral system could become a *real* and *very live* issue for voters.

The claim that 'ordinary people' are not concerned with constitutional issues is not only patronising, it is wrong-headed. Roy Hattersley's dismissal of constitutional issues because they are not 'bread and butter' is equally disingenuous. He knows perfectly well that it was not 'the people' who *originated* the demand for the vote in 1832, 1867 or 1884, but that once reform had been raised by radical political activists, including radical MPs, support was gathered and mobilised 'from below'. As Bernard Shaw rightly observed, it was not merely the great men who were responsible for these reforms. Of course issues of constitutional reform issues do not spring spontaneously from the everyday rhythms of work, home, food and play; but they are nonetheless capable of being 'popular' and 'vote-catching'.

The next general election campaign is indubitably the best opportunity we will have to raise electoral reform with voters. With tactical voting becoming ever more widespread, information will surface as to who is running second to Tory incumbents in the 100 or so constituencies where the national contest will really be decided. Voters in these key constituencies will be empowered to vote for the rest of us. They will decide our fate in their polling booths. We must hope they will do so pragmatically: that they use their vote so it counts.

If voters' imagination is captured by the failings of first-past-the-post at this crucial juncture, the Front Benches will find it difficult to ignore the voters' dilemma any longer. Is the election really the grand national contest in 634 seats (outside Northern Ireland) between the main parties which the media and politicians are promoting? Are supporters really marshalling to display their undying party allegiances?

Or is the election instead a very different affair – a scramble in less than 150 seats, the results of which are unpredictable precisely because voters are increasingly 'smart' and vote to take account of the unfairness of the electoral system?

If canvassers report that voters on their doorsteps are dissatisfied with the voting system, then political leaders will take notice. Voters who announce their intention to vote tactically and are unashamed of their own pragmatism will send a severe shock to the edifice of the political establishment. As Shaw concluded in 1892: 'No sensible man throws away a weapon which has won so much for those who have learned how to use it.'

Voters can effect change more surely and effectively than a whole raft of political lobbyists and and orchestrated campaigns inside the charmed circle of political activists. Ribble Valley showed that voters have indeed learned how to use their votes if they are given accurate information.

Like Robin Cook, I feel a sincere devotion to the House of Commons. I am attached to Parliament, and I am distressed by its increasingly obvious dismemberment from British society. I want to help place Westminster securely back on the trunk of its body politic, in its natural resting place. But to achieve electoral reform, it is first necessary to desire and promote it. We radicals have to take reform seriously before anyone else will. If reform is dismissed as a palliative and a sham by those on the left, then it will certainly always be put on the back-burner by the rest of the political establishment.

Supporters of electoral reform are vulnerable to a parallel negative pressure from another perspective. During the general election campaign, the pressure will be intense on Party supporters and activists to hunker down and close ranks. Party headquarters are understandably keen to 'fight the campaign' from the top downwards, and are also anxious to convey the picture that every candidate, member and lowly supporter professes unquestioning and undying allegiance to the Party cause. Paradoxically, this strategy is not going to win the contests in the crucial seats.

In these constituencies, the electoral arithmetic means that tactical voting, pragmatic approaches and support for electoral reform will be the real vote winners. Candidates who can think for themselves have already learned this lesson and are proclaiming their support for electoral reform and wooing tactical voters. They have learned to take voters seriously.

If the fall-out from the next general election does not provide the backdrop for the political drama of reforming the electoral system, then we will only have ourselves to blame. The times are most auspicious for unsettling the foundations of first-past-the-post. Voters have been undermining the system themselves, and they will do so in ever greater numbers this time round. We have to highlight their behaviour and draw the radical, pragmatic conclusions from it. We need to invite voters to realise their own power. History does not present such opportunities twice in a row. Our own minds and hearts have to concentrate on this matter at hand, for no one else's will.

6. Profiles of the Marginals

Profiles of the marginal seats are alphabetical within English region, and within Scotland and Wales. An index to all the constituency profiles is provided on page 155.

The Conservative majority given is for the 1987 general election. The first column gives the number of votes for each party in 1987 and the second column the percentage vote.

For an explanation of the 'category' given for each seat, please refer to Tim Johnson's 'Marginal Decisions' (chapter 3).

The following abbreviations are used:

Con for Conservative

Lab for Labour

SDP for Social Democratic Party

Lib for Liberal Party

Lib Dem for the Liberal Democrats (Formed just after the 1987 Election by the merger of the Liberals and the bulk of the SDP.)

SNP for Scottish National Party

PC for Plaid Cymru

Grn for the Green Party

Oth for Other candidates

PPC for Prospective Parliamentary Candidate ('Prospective' because candidates are not technically confirmed until the election date is decided. Where no PPC appears for a particular party it is because none had been selected at the time of going to press.)

Research was conducted, and profiles were written and compiled, by Gareth Smyth, Tim Johnson, Peter Hanington, Stuart Weir, Nina Fishman, Stephen Robinson and Seth Weir. Regional summaries by Gareth Smyth, except for Scotland by Peter Hanington.

LONDON

In 1987 there was a slight swing to the Conservatives in London, enough to gain three seats from Labour – Battersea, Walthamstow and Fulham. There are now 21 Conservative-held seats in the 'easier win' or 'Labour decider' categories, all theoretically seats Labour needs for an overall majority.

In the last set of London local government elections before the next general election, in May 1990, at its high point in the national opinion polls, Labour achieved a set of results ranging from the disastrous to the mildly encouraging. On the basis of those results, they would have gained only 15 of the 21, failing to win some seats with tiny Tory majorities, like Hornsey & Wood Green, Battersea and Westminster North. In addition they would have lost Tooting, Newham South, and nearly Brent East to the Conservatives. The Newham result was of particular concern as this working-class constituency, which had a Labour majority of nearly 13,000 in 1979, had seen a 9% swing to the Conservatives in 1987.

In addition Labour would have failed to win back Southwark & Bermondsey from Liberal Democrat MP Simon Hughes, and would have lost Bow & Poplar to the Liberal Democrats. Centre party interest will now centre on removing Mildred Gordon in Bow & Poplar, shoring up Simon Hughes, having another crack at Richmond & Barnes (possibly neighbouring Twickenham), and the uphill fight to save the two SDP seats of Greenwich and Woolwich.

The poor results of May 1990 produced a high-profile Labour inquest into its London campaigning structure. The proposed removal of the London General Secretary provoked Party organisers to threaten industrial action, and led, after many months, to an eventual fudge.

Labour's 'London problem' has basically two dimensions. First, demographic change has seen the skilled working class (traditionally the steadying backbone of the Party) moving out to the suburbs, leaving a population polarised between the better-off and the poor. Low voter registration as a result of the poll tax is prevalent in the last group, particularly among Afro-Carribeans. And some areas, including Battersea, Fulham and Putney (all target Labour seats) have visibly gentrified.

Second, some Labour Councils have pursued controversial policies on race, sexual equality and even international issues (to little practical avail), while at the same time failing to deliver traditional Council policies in an effective or efficient way. The Conservative 'flagships' of Wandsworth and Westminster have concentrated on basic policies like emptying bins and cleaning the streets and at the same time, with generous government grants, set a very low poll tax. The presence of the national media, and its London orientation, have ensured that the contrast between these Labour and Conservative Councils has been well aired.

Labour is attempting to counter the problem by shifting attention away from local Councils to London-wide issues like public transport, the Health Service and the need for a regional authority for the capital. In addition there is some polling evidence that voters are more likely to vote for Mr Kinnock than for their local Labour Council.

Tory Central Office's frequent dispatch of ministers for 'photo-opportunities' in Westminster and Wandsworth is not, however, simply the result of their great fondness for the two flagship boroughs. Central Office is well aware that London is a crucial battle-ground for the next election, a battle-ground that could be the key to maintaining a Conservative Government.

BATTERSEA

Con maj 857:

Con	20,945	44.2%
Lab	20,088	42.4%
SDP	5,634	11.9%

Swing required 0.9%. **Category** Labour easier win. **MP** John Bowis **Lab PPC** Alf Dubs **Lib Dem PPC** Roger O'Brien

Battersea – famous for its power station (unused for many years) and the celebrated dogs' home – is to be found just south of the Thames. In 1987, the constituency fell to Conservative insurance broker, John Bowis, on a 4.6% swing. Labour had held the seat, and its predecessor Battersea North, since 1935. No other constituency more graphically illustrates Labour's London problem.

Demographic change has favoured a long-term drift to the right. But 'yuppification' is accompanied by straightforward political factors. Tory-controlled Wandsworth Council was regarded as Mrs Thatcher's 'flagship' local authority, and while this has to a certain extent been 'hyped', the Council has concentrated on the efficient delivery of very visible services like cleaning the streets, and answering the phone at the Town Hall.

The contrast with neighbouring Labour-controlled Lambeth could not be more marked. Lambeth has an appalling public image of incompetence, political posturing, and dirty streets. And while Lambeth set one of the highest poll taxes in the country in 1990, Wandsworth set the lowest outside Scotland (£148). The argument that Lambeth provides a wider range of services, more nursery places, adult education etc, has some validity but has cut little ice with voters.

Consequently Labour was slaughtered in the 1990 local elections in Wandsworth, and on that result John Bowis would have held his seat with an increased majority of 14%. In 1991, Lambeth has seen screaming matches in the Council chamber over the Gulf War, the threatened return of former leader 'Red Ted' Knight, and a planned poll tax of nearly £600 (now capped by the Government). Meanwhile in Wandsworth, the Government switch to VAT for local government finance has meant residents will have to pay no poll tax at all!

Alf Dubs, former Battersea MP and reselected as PPC, has won many friends and wide respect over the years. But the omens for Labour in Battersea do not look good.

BRENTFORD & ISLEWORTH

Con maj 7,953:

Con	26,230	47.7%
Lab	18,277	33.2%
SDP	9,626	17.5%
Grn	849	1.5%

Swing required 7.8%. **Category** Labour decider. **MP** Barney Heyhoe **Lab PPC** Ann Kean

Brentford & Isleworth is a west London, socially-mixed seat running along the north bank of the Thames from Chiswick to the railway bridge by Richmond Old Deer Park. It coincides with the eastern half of the London borough of Hounslow, taking in half of Hounslow town centre.

The Labour-controlled Council has a reasonably good local profile and is generally regarded as mainstream. In the local elections of May 1990 Labour out-polled the Conservatives by 2.6% in Brentford & Isleworth.

Sir Barney Heyhoe first won the seat on its creation in February 1974. He is a colourful character on the 'wet' wing of the Conservative Party, commanding a personal vote. Labour's PPC Ann Kean contested the constituency unsuccessfully in 1987.

Ms Kean is the sister of Sylvia Heal MP, who won the 1990 Mid Stafforshire by-election for Labour. Her husband, Alan Kean, is standing in the neighbouring constituency of Feltham & Heston. The Keans are racing the Prentices (Gordon standing in Pendle, Bridget in Lewisham East) to be the first Labour married couple in the Commons.

CROYDON NORTH WEST

Con maj 3,988:

Con	18,665	47.0%
Lab	14,677	37.0%
Lib	6,363	16.0%

Swing required 5%. **Category** Labour decider. **MP** Humfrey Malins **Lab PPC** Malcolm Wicks

Croydon North West is the most socially mixed of the four constituencies in the generally well-to-do south London borough of Croydon. It was the scene in 1981 of a short-lived triumph for the Liberals, when Bill Pitt won a by-election at a time when Roy Jenkins' SDP was out to 'break the mould' of British politics.

Since then, the centre vote has consistently declined and Labour achieved a 4% swing from the Tories in 1987, a very good result in London terms. The local Liberal Democrats are in disarray and without a candidate at the time of going to press.

Labour's PPC Malcolm Wicks is an intelligent, witty, articulate reformist with a professional background in family policy. Incumbent Conservative since 1983 is Humfrey Malins, the son of an Anglican minister, a solicitor, and a low-profile MP.

Labour's local machine is well oiled and scored some success in the 1990 local elections. On that result Croydon North West would have produced a majority for Mr Wicks of 16.5%. If the 'loony left' factor stays at arms length, this looks like fertile ground for Mr Kinnock.

DULWICH

Con maj 180:

Con	16,563	42.4%
Lab	16,383	42.0%
SDP	5,664	14.5%
Grn	432	1.2%

Swing required 0.2%. **Category** Labour easier win. **MP** Gerald Bowden **Lab PPC** Tessa Jowell **Lib Dem PPC** Alex Goldie

An internal Labour Party report of mid-1990 described the image of Southwark Council as 'absolutely appalling'. The report went on to suggest that the northern end of the borough, Bermondsey (held by Liberal Democrat MP Simon Hughes), is particularly dependent on Council services, accounting for a drop in Labour's vote from 39% in the 1987 general election to 35% in the 1990 local elections.

In Dulwich, the more up-market southern end of the borough, Council services are less prominent, and here the Labour share of the vote rose to 50%.

The argument is simplified – picturesque Dulwich Village is far from typical of the seat as a whole – but it helps to explain why this must be regarded as Labour's most likely gain in London. Tessa Jowell is an able communicator, conscientious and photogenic. She has impeccable credentials as a moderate and no real connections with Southwark Council.

Some have suggested that the Green vote in 1987 cost Labour the seat. It is interesting then to note that the former Green candidate, Alex Goldie, is now set to stand for the Liberal Democrats. Whilst at time of writing Jonathon Porritt has not as yet followed him, this could introduce an interesting dimension to this environment-conscious seat.

EDMONTON

Con maj 7,286:

	Con	24,556	51.2%
	Lab	17,270	36.0%
	SDP	6,115	12.8%

Swing required 7.6%. **Category** Labour decider. **MP** Ian Twinn
Lab PPC Andy Love

Edmonton is to be found in the borough of Enfield on the way out to Essex. Previously Labour since 1935, it was captured for the Tories in 1983 by planning lecturer Dr Ian Twinn who went on to increase his majority in 1987 to its present comfortable state.

The constituency ranges from working-class areas in its east end, where the turn-out for elections tends to be low, to more salubrious residential areas in the north-west. It is interestingly surrounded by three constituencies of very varied characters: Enfield Southgate, true suburbia; Tottenham, held by Bernie Grant; and Chingford, home of 'Essex man' and Norman Tebbit MP, who is retiring from the Commons at the next election. And indeed, Edmonton shares characteristics with its neighbours – Tory commuters, a high proportion of ethnic minority voters who support Labour, and a white working class whose loyalties have tended to the Tories but whose support cannot be taken for granted.

Labour's PPC, Andy Love, is a 42 year-old Scot, down-to-earth but far from dour, and potentially an excellent MP. With a 7% margin of comfort in 1990's local elections, this looks a reasonable outside bet for Labour.

ELTHAM

Con maj 6,460:

	Con	19,752	47.5%
	Lab	13,292	32.0%
	Lib	8,542	20.5%

Swing required 7.7%. **Category** Labour decider. **MP** Peter Bottomley **Lab PPC** Clive Efford **Lib Dem PPC** Chris McGinty

Eltham is the southern swathe of the borough of Greenwich, where the two other 'SDP riviera' seats are set for a titanic clash between sitting Owenite MPs (Rosie Barnes and John Cartwright) and a resurgent Labour Party.

Eltham has changed hands between Labour and the Tories several times since the war. Its current MP is Peter Bottomley, whose wife Virginia represents South West Surrey. Mr Bottomley's relaxed style and assured television performances seem to suit the mood of the voters as he has held a comfortable majority since his first election at a by-election in 1975.

Mr Bottomley cannot, however, afford to be complacent. Labour has a solid base of support in the Council estates, and it uses its majority on the local authority to concentrate on delivering services rather than formulating foreign policy. PPC Clive Efford, a local cab driver in his 30s, has his campaign up and running on issues like education and NHS cutbacks. There is a significant centre vote of over 20% to be squeezed, and the outcome of the election here will depend at least in part on whether Mr Bottomley or Mr Efford manage that more effectively.

ERITH & CRAYFORD

Con maj 6,994:

Con	20,203	45.2%
Lab	13,209	29.5%
SDP	11,300	25.3%

Swing required 7.9%. **Category** Labour decider. **MP** David Evenett **Lab PPC** Nigel Beard **Lib Dem PPC** Masie Jamieson

As recently as 1979 Labour won over 50% in this consituency on the borders of London and Kent. The victor that year, James Wellbeloved subsequently joined the fledgling SDP, fought again and lost in 1983 to Lloyds underwiter David Evenett. Mr Evenett increased his majority substantially with a 3% swing, against the national trend and above any 'double incumbency' factor, in 1987.

The underlying process at work here is the erosion of traditional, unthinking Labour loyalties. The breakaway of the SDP, the growth of owner-occupation with Council-house right-to-buy, and disillusionment with some of Labour's national policies of the early 1980s, mean that voters here consider their best interests before marking their cross – a development also found in south-of-England marginals like Swindon, Slough and Harlow.

This suggests that, despite a strong Labour showing here in local elections, voter perception of the parties nationally, particularly on the management of the economy, may be the crucial factor. And on that, Labour still has some way to go.

FELTHAM & HESTON

Con maj 5,430:

Con 27,755 46.5%
Lab 22,325 37.4%
SDP 9,623 16.1%

Swing required 4.6%. **Category** Labour easier win. **MP** Patrick Ground **Lab PPC** Alan Keen **Lib Dem PPC** Mike Hoban

Feltham & Heston is the western end of the borough of Hounslow, one of the more successful Labour-run Councils. It has a large working-class and Asian population, and is also verging on the M4 corridor.

Mortgage interest rates are likely to be an important issue here, both for those who have bought their Council homes and for the first-time buyers living in the new privately-owned houses in Heston. Similarly, the employment situation shows signs of deterioration, with lay-offs at Heathrow Airport and Aerospace, both important local employers. These factors exemplify the importance for Mr Major to get the economy right before the election.

Patrick Ground, a barrister specialising in planning, is regarded as personable and is liked even by political opponents. He has, however, had a relatively low profile in local newspapers since becoming MP in 1983, and this may be important in a large constituency with over 80,000 electors. Mr Keen was selected relatively late by Labour, as overspill politics from the Punjab have created some difficulties for the local Party. Mike Hoban is proving himself an energetic campaigner for the Liberals (among other things dragging shopping trollies out of Feltham pond). Mr Hoban may be a name to watch for the future, and could complicate the Labour/Conservative battle.

Feltham & Heston is just within the Labour easier win category, and as such a crucial seat to watch.

FULHAM

Con maj 6,322:

Con 21,752 51.8%
Lab 15,430 36.7%
SDP 4,365 10.4%
Grn 465 1.1%

Swing required 7.6%. **Category** Labour decider. **MP** Matthew Carrington **Lab PPC** Nick Moore

In 1986 Nick Raynsford snatched Fulham from the Conservatives by 3,000 votes in a sensational Labour by-election victory, only to lose the seat in the general election a year later. Mr Raynsford has now moved off to fight the SDP's Rosie Barnes in

Greenwich, and Labour's new PPC, Nick Moore, cannot hope to match his high profile.

This might suggest that Labour is not likely to win the seat. Demographic change has not been to their advantage. The Fulham held by Michael Stewart, the former Labour Foreign Secretary, between 1955 and 1979, was decidedly less fashionable and 'yuppified' than the Fulham of today.

Labour will draw comfort, however, with the 4% swing from 1987 achieved in the 1990 local elections, despite the loss of seats across the borough. Labour's Walworth Road Headquarters still think they can win Fulham as it remains on their private list of target seats.

The sitting MP Matthew Carrington will benefit from 'double incumbency' – the advantage that comes to a sitting MP at the end of his first term. Fulham remains an interesting paradox: a seat that Mr Kinnock's modernised Party should be able to win if returning to Government, but one that looks a hard nut to crack.

HAMPSTEAD & HIGHGATE

Con maj 2,221:

Con	19,236	42.5%
Lab	17,015	37.6%
SDP	8,744	19.3%

Swing required 2.9%. **Category** Labour easier win. **MP** Sir Geoffrey Finsberg (retiring) **Con PPC** Oliver Letwin **Lab PPC** Glenda Jackson **Lib Dem PPC** David Wrede

Gerry Isaaman, editor of the local *Hampstead & Highgate Express* is gleefully rubbing his hands at the prospect of this contest. In the red corner Glenda Jackson who (as they say) needs no introduction; in the blue corner Oliver Letwin who helped invent the poll tax in Mrs Thatcher's Policy Unit. And into the fray for the Liberal Democrats David Wrede, member of the Royal College of Surgeons and archetypical, articulate young doctor.

The world's media will descend for the campaign and a by-election atmosphere should quickly develop. There are plenty of local issues – the opting out of the Royal Free Hospital, the record of Labour-controlled Camden Council, the infamous Northern underground line, and the vexed question of whether a MacDonalds should be allowed in Hampstead High Street.

Contrary to popular perception, Hampstead & Highgate is a socially-mixed seat. It ranges from the eastern end of Kilburn (dubbed Ireland's 33rd county) and the tower blocks of Swiss Cottage to the leafy surrounds of Hampstead Heath and Belsize Village. Labour have made it clear they intend to play for the centre ground, partly explaining their choice of Ms Jackson who is strong on sensitive issues like defence and a signatory of Charter 88.

Ringside seats should be booked early.

HAYES & HARLINGTON

Con maj 5,965:   Con 21,355 49.2%

                        Lab 15,390 35.5%

                        SDP 6,641   15.3%

Swing required 6.9%. **Category** Labour decider. **MP** Terry Dicks
Lab PPC John McDonnell **Lib Dem PPC** Tony Little

Hayes & Harlington is very much a working-class constituency. Formerly industrial, it is now predominantly service-oriented. Thorn EMI and Heathrow Airport are major employers.

Its MP Terry Dicks was first elected in 1983, a direct result of the sitting Labour member Neville Sanderson defecting to the SDP and drawing away Labour voters. In 1987 the Labour candidate was involved in a much-publicised court case and Mr Dicks increased his majority to nearly 6,000.

Terry Dicks is an outspoken right-winger always keen to speak in immigration debates. The prospective Labour candidate this time round, the former local GLC Councillor, John McDonnell regards Dicks as 'the Le Pen of Hayes' who concentrates on 'rent-a-gob stuff in the media'. Recent allegations that Mr Dicks visited Baghdad in 1988 as guest of Saddam Hussein's Government are likely to damage an MP whose appeal has always been based on populism.

Labour out-polled the Tories by 16.5% in the May 1990 local elections. A very lively tussle and close result seem to be on the cards.

HORNSEY & WOOD GREEN

Con maj 1,179:   Con 25,397 43.0%

                        Lab 23,618 40.0%

                        SDP 8,928   15.1%

                        Grn 1,154   2.0%

Swing required 1.5%. **Category** Labour easier win. **MP** Hugh Rossi **Lab PPC** Barbara Roche

Hornsey & Wood Green is a large constituency taking in Muswell Hill (including Alexandra Palace), Crouch End, part of Highgate and Wood Green. It swung to Labour in 1987 and has now the third smallest Tory majority in London.

The local Council, Haringey, has received much tabloid publicity of the 'loony left' variety. There have been bitter battles within the local Labour Party in which the hard left has generally come off the loser, and the Council has of late tried to concentrate on improving service delivery.

The highest poll tax in the country was instrumental in Labour's poor showing in the local elections on May 1990, and on the basis of that result Hornsey & Wood Green would remain Conservative.

The Liberal Democrats, though without a PPC at the time of writing, should see some potential in this kind of seat. Mr Rossi has a high local profile and as MP since 1966 is well established. Barbara Roche, set to fight the seat for a second time, will need to appeal to the centre ground if she is to win.

ILFORD SOUTH

Con maj 4,572:

Con	20,351	48.4%
Lab	15,779	37.5%
Lib	5,928	14.1%

Swing required 5.5%. **Category** Labour decider. **MP** Neil Thorne **Lab PPC** Mike Gapes **Lib Dem PPC** George Hogarth

Ilford South is a classic ding-dong marginal which has bounced backwards and forwards, at least until 1979 when it was gained by chartered surveyor Neil Thorne at his second attempt. The constituency is a kind of no-man's land between London and Essex. Unlike Barking and Dagenham to the south, and Romford to the east, it has a significant ethnic minority population (20% in the 1981 census), a characteristic shared with Newham to the west.

With a significant proportion of down-market terraced housing and little civic identity (Redbridge is the London borough no-one seems to have heard of!), this is the sort of constituency that could shift to Labour on a national swing. This will suit their PPC, the cheery, bespectacled Mike Gapes, International Officer at Labour's Walworth Road HQ, who will be bidding to change his backroom role in shaping Labour's post-unilateralist defence policy for the up-front role of MP.

KENSINGTON

Con maj 4,447:

Con	14,818	47.5%
Lab	10,317	33.2%
SDP	5,379	17.2%
Grn	528	1.7%
Oth	95	0.3%

Swing required 7.7%. **Category** Labour decider. **MP** Dudley Fishburn **Lab PPC** Ann Holmes **Lib Dem PPC** Chris Shirley

Kensington is one of the smallest constituencies in the country, both in terms of its size and electorate. It is also one of the most polarised – the affluence of its southern half (Holland Park, Kensington Palace Gardens) contrasts with the more socially down-at-heel neighbourhoods at the top of Ladbroke Grove.

From February 1974 until his death in 1988, Kensington was represented by Sir Brandon Rhys Williams, a popular Tory 'wet' who defied the Party whip over child benefit and was widely regarded as an excellent constituency MP. The subsequent by-election turned out to be very close, Dudley Fishburn holding off a challenge from Labour's Ann Holmes by only 815 votes.

In itself this result may have convinced Labour-leaning voters that the seat can be won. Sir Brandon is a hard act to follow, and Mr Fishburn has made a limited impact. The husky-voiced Ann Holmes is charismatic and forceful, so a lively campaign seems likely. In the local elections of May 1990 Labour out-polled the Conservatives 45%-42.5% with the centre vote collapsing.

LEWISHAM EAST

Con maj 4,814:

Con	19,873	45.1%
Lab	15,059	34.2%
SDP	9,118	20.7%

Swing required 5.5%. **Category** Labour decider. **MP** Colin Moynihan **Lab PPC** Bridget Prentice **Lib Dem PPC** Julian Hawkins

The fresh-faced Colin Moynihan is a former Oxford rowing blue (a cox) who bumped sitting Labour MP Roland Moyle in 1983 and took a clearer lead over Labour in 1987.

Lewisham East tends to flow with the national tide, as one might expect for a constituency which varies from the 'villagey' Blackheath to the massive Downham Council estate.

Launched for Labour is teacher Bridget Prentice, hoping to form a parliamentary 'pair' with her husband Gordon, who is standing in Pendle in Lancashire. While there is still a significant centre presence, the contest in Lewisham East, like the annual Varsity encounter on the Thames, looks like a two-boat race.

LEWISHAM WEST

Con maj 3,772:

Con	20,995	46.2%
Lab	17,223	37.9%
Lib	7,247	15.9%

Swing required 5.2%. **Category** Labour easier win. **MP** John Maples **Lab PPC** Jim Dowd **Lib Dem PPC** Eileen Neale

Lewisham West looks a marginally better bet for Labour than Lewisham East, though both would have been captured on the 1990 local results. Cambridge and Harvard Business School educated John Maples took the seat in 1983 from Labour's Christopher Price, who himself had taken it from John Gummer in the days before Mr Gummer headed for the beautiful Suffolk coast and 'mad cow disease' became national headline news.

The constituency ranges from the seedy borders of Deptford to the leafy borders of Bromley commuterland. Labour's Jim Dowd, planning to contest the seat for a seond time, has been a local Councillor for nearly 20 years though he is only just 40. Mr Dowd, a telephone engineer, is keen to put the health service at the centre of political debate, especially as the local hospital is 'opting out'.

There is an interesting contrast of style between the two major parties' prospective candidates, so this should be an interesting contest.

MITCHAM & MORDEN

Con maj 6,183:

Con 23,002	48.2%
Lab 16,819	35.2%
SDP 7,930	16.6%

Swing required 6.5%. **Category** Labour decider. **MP** Angela Rumbold **Lab PPC** Siobhain McDonagh **Lib Dem PPC** John Field

A Conservative seat since the by-election of 1982, Mitcham & Morden is tending towards Labour. High mortgage rates are punishing first-time buyers, the popular local Wilson Hospital has been shut, and as an outer London seat it is relatively unaffected by Labour's 'London factor'.

Mitcham & Morden is part of Merton, the only Council Labour gained in London in May 1990. Despite a planned poll tax increase of over £100 for 1991/2, the Council has maintained a reasonable profile.

Labour's Siobhain McDonagh, who has always lived locally, describes herself as 'very uncontroversial really'. Despite Ms Rumbold's prominence as one of the leading Conservative women who weren't included in Mr Major's first all-male cabinet, this looks Labour's best chance of gaining a 'decider seat' in the capital.

PUTNEY

Con maj 6,907:

Con 24,197	50.5%
Lab 17,290	36.1%
Lib 5,934	12.4%
Grn 508	1.1%

Swing required 7.2%. **Category** Labour decider. **MP** David Mellor **Lab PPC** Judith Chegwidden **Lib Dem PPC** John Martyn

Putney has been gentrifying over a long period. It has swung further and further to the Conservatives since David Mellor first became MP. Mr Mellor has entered the cabinet as Treasury Chief Secretary and appears a rising television star in Mr Major's Government. Local Conservative confidence will have been further boosted with the crushing victory in the 1990 Wandsworth Council elections.

Labour's Walworth Road HQ has apparently given up the ghost, removing Putney from its list of 'target marginals'. Minerals consultant Judith Chegwidden is untainted by any connection with Labour's hard left, strongly critical of inefficiency in the neighbouring borough of Lambeth, and a supporter of electoral reform. If such a candidate cannot seriously dent Mr Mellor's majority this time round, Putney will have to be regarded as a safe Conservative seat.

RICHMOND & BARNES

Con maj 1,766:

Con	21,729	47.7%
Lib	19,903	43.8%
Lab	3,227	7.1%
Grn	610	1.3%

Swing required 1.9%. **Category** Liberal Democrat target. **MP** Jeremy Hanley **Lib Dem PPC** Jenny Tonge

The Liberals have dominated local government in the borough of Richmond throughout the 1980s, winning 48 out of 52 seats in 1990, but the parliamentary seat of Richmond & Barnes has eluded their grasp. In 1983 Jeremy Hanley became MP with a majority of only 74. In 1987 the success of the Kinnock/Mandelson campaign may have frightened Liberal-inclined Tories to return to the fold: this, with the advantage of incumbency, gave Mr Hanley an increased majority of nearly 2,000.

Voters here would seem to value the excellent schools and 'green' policies of their Liberal Council whilst plumping for a Conservative Government at Westminster.

A Councillor for ten years, Jenny Tonge may have been chosen in the hope that Council successes will 'rub off' on the Liberal's parliamentary candidate. She is very much the 'local candidate' – her home is in Kew – but is also a committed European, delighted that her daughter is studying at Nice University. As a doctor and former Chair of Social Services, she is strong on 'caring' issues but also keen to argue the case for an independent central Bank.

Dr Tonge is also radiant and personable, a suitable foil for Mr Hanley, who, as well having a reputation for hard work, is a handsome and accomplished TV performer. A contest to *watch*!

STREATHAM

Con maj 2,407:		
	Con 18,916	44.9%
	Lab 16,509	39.2%
	Lib 6,663	15.8%

Swing required 2.9%. **Category** Labour easier win. **MP** Sir William Shelton **Lab PPC** Keith Hill **Lib Dem PPC** John Pindar

Streatham is the south-west third of the Labour-controlled borough of Lambeth, which has a disastrous public profile. The seat would have stayed Tory on the 1990 local results, and Lambeth's antics over the Gulf War were followed by a projected poll tax of nearly £600. It remains to be seen whether the belated intervention of Labour's national Party can repair the situation.

Nevertheless, in Streatham the demographic trend is in Labour's favour. The Afro-Caribbean population has been moving up the hill from Brixton, and many well-to-do families have moved to outer London to be replaced by first-time buyers finding it hard to pay the mortgage.

Labour have selected a local candidate with no Council connections: Keith Hill is a public critic of the hard left, a supporter of PR, and a member of 'Friends of the Earth' and 'Greenpeace'. It should be an interesting campaign.

WALTHAMSTOW

Con maj 1,512:		
	Con 13,748	39.0%
	Lab 12,236	34.7%
	SDP 8,852	25.1%

Swing required 2.2%. **Category** Labour easier win. **MP** Hugo Summerson **Lab PPC** Neil Gerrard **Lib Dem PPC** Peter Leighton

Walthamstow is a mainly working-class constituency which was moving to the Tories by more than the national swing in 1979 and 1983. In 1986 a mild 'loony left' factor was introduced when Labour gained control of Waltham Forest Council and proceeded to boost the rates bill, a similar process to that in Ealing and Hammersmith & Fulham in the same year.

When Walthamstow's Labour MP Eric Deakin was unseated in the 1987 general election, the constituency became an oft-quoted example of Labour's 'London factor'. His replacement, the articulate Hugo Summerson has rapidly established himself as an assiduous constituency MP, keen to take up issues like overactive burglar alarms and poor TV reception which appear trivial to those who don't experience them.

Despite growing unemployment, increased homelessness and local controversy over road plans, Mr Summerson – especially with the effect of 'double incumbency' – will be difficult to shift. It is slightly surprising therefore that – contrary to Labour thinking in Dulwich, Streatham and Hampstead & Highgate – Labour have selected a PPC with a strong Council connection. Neil Gerrard is a well-known local figure and his attention to local concerns has won respect. But he was Council leader at the time of the rate increases that were instrumental in handing Mr Summerson the seat in the first place. Labour will have to hope that local voters have short memories.

WESTMINSTER NORTH

Con maj 3,310:

Con	19,941	47.3%
Lab	16,631	39.5%
SDP	5,116	12.1%
Grn	450	1.1%

Swing required 3.9%. **Category** Labour easier win. **MP** John Wheeler **Lab PPC** Jenny Edwards **Lib Dem PPC** Justin Wigoder

John Wheeler first won the old Paddington seat from Labour in 1979, held it narrowly in 1983 and more comfortably in 1987.

Two factors appear to be working in his favour. First, a substantial number of voters have 'vanished' from the electoral register (more than 21,000 in the City of Westminster between 1984 and February 1991) – leading to Labour accusations of political gerrymandering.

Second, despite controversy surrounding Westminster City Council's sale of three cemeteries for 15p, the Conservatives achieved a landslide victory in the local elections of May 1990.

In fact, the Conservative 'surge' was achieved largely at the expense of the Liberal Democrats, and although Labour would not have won Westminster North on those results, there was a slight Conservative-to-Labour swing in the constituency.

Labour are well-organised in Westminster North. Their prospective candidate Jenny Edwards, who stood in 1979, is a political adviser to Labour front-bencher Jo Richardson MP. John Wheeler has assumed a growing prominence as Chairman of the Parliamentary Home Affairs Committee and is an unoffical, but effective, television spokesman for the Conservatives in London.

On the 1987 statistics, Westminster North is the 43rd most-vulnerable-to-Labour Conservative seat in the country. In practice, its capture is likely to prove difficult.

MIDLANDS

The Midlands, sandwiched between the Conservative South and the Labour North, is often regarded as the key to the outcome of the general election. This is a simplified but nonetheless graphic view. In fact, the Midlands present a complex picture.

In 1987 Labour made only limited progress in the East Midlands, partly because of the damage done by the split in the Miners' Union, and Labour's sole gains were Nottingham North, Leicester South and Leicester East. Lincoln produced a very close approximation of the overall national result.

Slightly more progress was made in the West Midlands, with the Birmingham seats swinging to Labour by generally 1-3%, and Coventry by around 3%, but this was not enough for Labour to make any actual gains in either of these cities. Tory Maureen Hicks snatched Wolverhampton North East, a splendid personal result which added to Labour's woes. In the research for this book, we found the West Midlands Regional Office of the Labour Party surprisingly unco-operative – their suspicion perhaps implying a nervousness about the election.

Derbyshire was more mixed in 1987, with swings to the Conservatives in three important marginals gained in 1983 (Amber Valley, Derbyshire South and Derby North), and very small pro-Labour swings where they occurred. This suggests an underlying, general shift to the right, making management of the economy perhaps the important national issue for Derbyshire voters.

The centre parties have never made a major breakthrough in the Midlands as a whole. Liberal Democrat attention will need to concentrate on areas nearer the Welsh border, Hereford representing their best bet in the region, with Wyre Forest an outside chance.

In Staffordshire in 1987 Labour's small favourable swing was nowhere near enough to take Burton, and they lost ground in Cannock & Burntwood. 1990 saw the dramatic success at the Mid Staffordshire by-election at the time of a massive national lead in the opinion polls for Mr Kinnock. Labour cannot expect anything like such a walkover, either in Mid Staffs or elsewhere, in this region come the general election.

AMBER VALLEY

Con maj 9,500:

Con	28,603	51.4%
Lab	19,103	34.4%
Lib	7,904	14.2%

Swing required 8.5%. **Category** Labour decider. **MP** Phillip Oppenheim **Lab PPC** John Cooper

The seat runs along the eastern bank of the Derwent, north of Derby – pretty countryside where it has not been blighted by industrial villages and small towns. Enough new industry has arrived to offset the worst of the losses from declining textile and small-scale manufacturing industries.

The performance of the Labour County Council, painted as high-spending and hard-line, is an issue in all the Derbyshire seats. But it is particularly acute in Amber Valley because the Labour candidate in 1983 and 1987 was David Bookbinder, the able but controversial leader of the Council since 1981. Phillip Oppenheim won the seat for the Tories in 1983 and went on to achieve one of the biggest pro-Tory swings in the 1987 election, 5.3%. He was helped by a collapse in the Alliance vote as well as the 'double incumbency' effect.

There is no reason to expect these special factors to give Mr Oppenheim any more help next time, so the seat will probably swing in line with the national average.

BIRMINGHAM HALL GREEN

Con maj 7,621:

Con	20,478	44.9%
Lab	12,857	28.2%
SDP	12,323	27.0%

Swing required 8.4%. **Category** Labour decider. **MP** Andrew Hargreaves **Lab PPC** Jane Slowey **Lib Dem PPC** David McGrath

Capture of Birmingham Hall Green would bring Labour to the brink of an overall majority (on the rather improbable assumption that they win every Conservative seat with a smaller percentage majority). The nature of the constituency demonstrates the hill Labour have to climb: it is a suburban area on the south-west fringe of the city, overwhelmingly owner-occupied and overwhelmingly white.

Eton and Oxford-educated, former fine art auctioneer with Christies, Andrew Hargreaves is articulate, intelligent and young (mid 30s). Hall Green was the strongest showing for the Alliance in the West Midlands, an area where they have so far failed to break through the two party battle. The nature of this seat suggests that it may continue to be relatively fertile ground in a general election, though it is not clear whether this is likely to damage Labour or the Tories more.

BIRMINGHAM NORTHFIELD

Con maj 3,135:

Con 24,024 45.1%
Lab 20,889 39.2%
SDP 8,319 15.6%

Swing required 3.0%. **Category** Labour easier win. **MP** Roger King **Lab PPC** Richard Burden

Benefiting from the 'double incumbency' effect, Roger King increased his share of the vote by 2.4% in this south-west Birmingham constituency which contains the Rover Longbridge factory and many of its workers. The Labour candidate, then, John Spellar (who had held the seat, briefly, between a by-election success in 1982 and the 1983 election) increased his share of the vote by only 1.7% and retired from the fray.

The electoral arithmetic of Northfield is close, but a Labour victory here will depend on voters returning to traditional loyalties in more convincing numbers in a seat once seen as a Labour stronghold. The old assumption that 'if the seat is working-class, then it will be Labour' no longer holds in the West Midlands. There is still a centre vote which could be eroded by the other parties, depending on voter perception of national campaigns and of the economy. This is an important test of Labour's new look under Mr Kinnock.

BIRMINGHAM SELLY OAK

Con maj 2,584:

Con 23,305 44.2%
Lab 20,721 39.3%
Lib 8,128 15.4%

Swing required 2.5%. **Category** Labour easier win. **MP** Anthony Beaumont-Dark **Lab PPC** Lynne Jones **Lib Dem PPC** David Osborne

Birmingham Selly Oak voters are a cross-section of the city's electorate: remnants of an older Tory loyalist area are now interspersed with areas of non-white immigrants nearer the city centre.

Lynne Jones may have an easier task to defeat the incumbent Conservative MP than her colleagues in the other Birmingham 'marginals' of Yardley and Northfield. In a year that was disappointing for Labour in the city, their vote increased by 4.9% in 1987, with the Liberals declining by 5.3%. The long-term trend here appears to be in Labour's favour, and stockbroker Anthony Beaumont-Dark is unlikely to survive.

BIRMINGHAM YARDLEY

Con maj 2,522:	Con 17,931	42.6%
	Lab 15,409	36.6%
	Lib 8,734	20.8%

Swing required 3%. **Category** Labour easier win. **MP** David Gilroy Beavan **Lab PPC** Estelle Morris **Lib Dem PPC** John Hemming

A Labour seat from 1945 until 1959, since then this constituency on the south-east outskirts of the city has been won by the party which won the general election as a whole. It is a classic, mainly skilled working-class Conservative/Labour marginal.

The MP since 1979, former city councillor and estate agent/surveyor David Gilroy Bevan, adheres to decidedly rightwing views. While the Liberal Democrats currently hold two out of the three city Council wards in Yardley, the Labour PPC, Estelle Morris (a teacher), is personable and politically proficient. This will be an important test for the 'electability' of new-look Labour.

BURTON

Con maj 9,830:	Con 29,160	50.7%
	Lab 19,330	33.6%
	Lib 9,046	15.7%

Swing required 8.6%. **Category** Labour decider. **MP** Ivan Lawrence **Lab PPC** Patricia Muddyman

Burton itself is a working-class brewing town not so much on the banks as in the flood plain of the River Trent. Testimony to the strong links between the beverage industry and the Tory Party is the fact that the seat has been firmly Tory for a long time. Its combination with a wide swathe of rural east Staffordshire is the other part of the story.

But increasing industrialisation in small towns like Uttoxeter and Rocester is changing the mix of voters and puts Labour in with a chance. Ivan Lawrence won on a smaller share of the vote in 1987 than he got in 1979. This should be one place where Labour is running with the current.

CANNOCK & BURNTWOOD

Con maj 2,689:	Con 24,186	44.5%
	Lab 21,497	39.5%
	Lib 8,698	16.0%

Swing required 2.5%. **Category** Labour easier win. **MP** Gerald Howarth **Lab PPC** Tony Wright

Gerald Howarth achieved a good result by holding Cannock & Burntwood in 1987, when he achieved a slight swing on the result that first brought him to Parliament in 1983. The seat should switch to Labour fairly easily given Labour's recovery since then, but PPC Tony Wright, fighting for the first time is taking nothing for granted and is campaigning vigorously.

The Liberal vote in 1987 fell by 6%, so it is interesting to note that one of Mr Wright's early press releases stressed his strong commitment to electoral reform, which may mean he is better placed to exploit any further decline in centre support than Mr Howarth, who is very much on the rightwing of the Conservative Party.

The constituency contains a solid Labour core, mining communities without working pits, as well as the commuter belt of '021s' who drive and entrain to Birmingham daily. (The fate of public tansport is one of Mr Wright's campaigning points.)

COVENTRY SOUTH WEST

Con maj 3,210:		
	Con 22,318	43.3%
	Lab 19,108	37.0%
	Lib 10,166	19.7%

Swing required 3.2%. **Category** Labour easier win. **MP** John Butcher **Lab PPC** Robert Slater

Coventry is a Labour City. Captured by John Butcher in 1979, South West is the only one of its four parliamentary seats which is held by the Conservatives.

A recent survey carried out by the Labour-controlled City Council suggested that 62% of residents were 'fairly' or 'very satisfied' with its services. Although the Militant Tendency has traditionally been strong in Coventry, this is unlikely to be seriously detrimental to Labour as their MP for South East, Dave Nellist, has emerged as hard-working and uncontroversial.

Three-quarters of the housing in South West is owner-occupied, but although this *is* the most affluent part of the city, the seat is not as middle-class as the statistic might suggest. South West used to contain the now-defunct Triumph car works, which remained the site for Rover Group headquarters (until their move to Solihull was announced in March 1991).

The City Council has proposed the establishment of a tram link from the city centre to Warwick University campus. An alleged 'threat to the character' of Earlsden, through which trams would pass, has seen John Butcher join local residents in voicing opposition.

Labour's Robert Slater, an FE lecturer, fought the seat in 1987 when he achieved a tiny swing of less than 1%. Mr Slater, who is apparently known as 'the suit' within the local Party, refused to talk to Common Voice without prior sanction from

Labour's Regional Office. He will need to shake off this mild paranoia in time for the general election if Labour are to gain the seat.

DERBY NORTH

Con maj 6,280:

Con 26,516	48.9%
Lab 20,236	37.2%
Lib 7,268	13.5%
Grn 291	0.5%

Swing required 5.9%. **Category** Labour decider. **MP** Gregory Knight **Lab PPC** Bob Laxton

Having just hung onto this seat in 1979, Labour's Philip Whitehead was swept away by the 1983 landslide to the Tories. He failed to win it back in 1987, with a 2.4% swing against him, about typical for the 'double incumbency' effect.

The seat is the rather more up-market, residential side of Derby. Allestree and other well-tended suburbs are now Tory strongholds. But with cut-backs at major Derby employers, such as Rolls Royce which is badly hit by the airline slump, there will be considerable anxiety behind the pampas grass and net curtains. Against an undistinguished sitting MP, Labour should be able to do at least as well here as its national average.

DERBYSHIRE SOUTH

Con maj 10,311:

Con 31,927	49.1%
Lab 21,616	33.2%
SDP 11,509	17.7%

Swing required 8%. **Category** Labour decider. **MP** Edwina Currie **Lab PPC** Mark Todd

With its power stations strung out along the Trent valley, this may be the constituency with most cooling towers per voter. Its scrubby countryside, closed-down coal towns and grimy industrial villages do not make it look like natural Tory territory.

Much of the seat was in the former Belper constituency, held for many years by George Brown, Deputy Leader of the Labour Party in the 1960s. But the Tories gained Belper in 1979, and Edwina Currie, the salmonella lady, has been ensconced in Derbyshire South since it was created in 1983.

Not only does Mrs Currie have her undoubted energy and talent for publicity in her favour, but the constituency also has some significant economic growth points. The most prominent is the new Toyota factory, just south-west of Derby. Credit for attracting this to the area is a predictable bone of contention between Mrs Currie and Derbyshire's firmly Labour County Council. Even if the national swing is big enough to unseat her, Mrs Currie should be able to summon up enough extra support to hold on against anything short of a landslide.

DUDLEY WEST

Con maj 13,808:

Con	32,224	49.8%
Lab	21,980	34.0%
Lib	10,477	16.2%

Swing required 7.5%. **Category** Labour decider. **MP** John Blackburn **Lab PPC** Kevin Lomax **Lib Dem PPC** Gerry Lewis

Dudley West had a Labour MP as late as 1979, but since his election that year former policeman John Blackburn has built up his majority to nearly 14,000. The growth of new, affluent housing estates seem to have moved the seat rightwards.

While there are some solid Labour wards, their votes alone are not enough to tip the balance, and there seems to be a psephological consensus that for Dudley West to leave the Tory stable would require a 'very good year indeed' for Labour.

Mr Blackburn is perhaps best known for his campaign against obscene publications and he seems likely to be able to continue his efforts from Westminster.

EREWASH

Con maj 9,754:

Con	28,775	48.6%
Lab	19,021	32.1%
SDP	11,442	19.3%

Swing required 8.3%. **Category** Labour decider. **MP** Peter Rost (retiring) **Con PPC** Angela Knight **Lab PPC** Sean Stanford

Erewash embraces a heavily built-up area between Derby and Nottingham, including the towns of Ilkeston and Long Eaton. Full of middling people and middling industry, it is just the kind of constituency which Labour must win to have a prospect of forming the Government. In fact, Labour will be helped to do better than average here by several factors.

Peter Rost, who has represented this seat and its predecessor, Derbyshire South East, since 1970 is retiring at the next election. Labour also suffered badly from the intervention of an Independent Labour candidate in 1983, and one of the best Alliance performances in this part of the country. It had still not recovered fully by 1987. The 1984-5 Miners' Strike and the UDM split may also have been a factor in a seat which borders the Nottinghamshire coalfield.

Unless the Conservatives are well ahead in the opinion polls, Angela Wright will do well to join her neighbouring fellow-woman Conservative Edwina Currie in the Commons.

HEREFORD

Con maj 1,413:

Con	24,865	47.5%
Lib	23,452	44.8%
Lab	4,031	7.7%

Swing required 1.4%. **Category** Liberal Democrat target. **MP** Colin Shepherd **Lib Dem PPC** Gwynoro Jones **Lab PPC** Ms J. Kelly

The constituency of Hereford comprises the town itself, which is surprisingly industrial, and rural areas like the Ross and Wye valleys. It has been held by the Conservatives consistently since the war, but has never been entirely safe.

The Liberals had effectively supplanted Labour as the main opposition between the mid-1960s and mid-70s, and the Labour vote has been squeezed back to under 10%. The Liberal Democrats are also strong in local government.

Colin Shepherd has mixed a practical interest in industry – through involvement with an engineering firm at Ross-on-Wye – with parliamentary involvement in agricultural issues. MP since 1974 and still in his early 50s, Mr Shepherd will offer stiff resistance, especially in farming country, and the Liberal Democrats will need further national improvement to topple him.

LEICESTERSHIRE NORTH WEST

Con maj 7,028:

Con	27,872	47.6%
Lab	20,044	34.3%
Lib	10,034	17.1%
Grn	570	1.0%

Swing required 6.7%. **Category** Labour decider. **MP** David Ashby **Lab PPC** David Taylor **Lib Dem PPC** Jeremy Beckett

Ten years ago there were around ten pits in the North West Leicestershire coalfield. The last one, Bagworth, shut in early 1991.

The town of Coalville and villages like Thringstone and Ellistown retain the character of mining communities, but this is far from being a depressed ex-mining area. The East Midlands Airport is a major employer; United Biscuits have a factory at Ashby; and there is a scattering of textiles, quarrying and open-cast working.

David Taylor is in many ways an ideal candidate for Labour. Born and bred in the constituency and with four children at local schools, he is a finance/computing manager at Leicestershire County Hall. Very much within the Labour mainstream, he may have the right credentials to win back the skilled workers who plumped for London barrister David Ashby in 1983 and 1987.

Liberal strength in the constituency can be found around Ashby, but their prospective candidate Jeremy Beckett lives in Derbyshire. Taylor will need to squeeze the centre vote and his support for PR may help.

LINCOLN

Con maj 7,483:

Con	27,097	46.5%
Lab	19,614	33.7%
SDP	11,319	19.4%

Swing required 6.4%. **Category** Labour decider. **MP** Kenneth Carlisle **Lab PPC** Nick Butler **Lib Dem PPC** David Harding-Price

Lincoln was originally a Celtic settlement called Lindon, 'the hill fort by a pool'. Its cathedral is the third largest in England exceeded only by St Pauls and York Minster.

Lincoln hit national political headlines in 1973 with Dick Taverne's defection from Labour to form his own Democratic Labour group, but memories of those traumas are fading for Labour. Their PPC Nick Butler played a leading if unsung role in the development of Labour's post-unilateralist defence policy, and he fought with energy and acumen in 1987, when the SDP vote dipped below the national average. (Lincoln had been an uncannily accurate microcosm of the aggregated national vote in 1983.)

Labour are back in firm control of a City Council where once Mr Taverne's group held considerable sway, and Mr Butler is concentrating his efforts on the four wards outside the city where there is still a Liberal Democrat presence. This is a seat where the cold numbers give a more pessimistic picture for Labour than the human heat which will be generated in the actual contest. Mr Butler has a good chance of removing Kenneth Carlisle, who on his election in 1979 had become the first Conservative MP for Lincoln since 1935!

NOTTINGHAM EAST

Con maj 456:

Con	20,162	42.9%
Lab	19,706	42.0%
Lib	6,887	14.7%
Oth	212	0.5%

Swing required 0.5%. **Category** Labour easier win. **MP** Michael Knowles

The Labour Party has an unhappy recent history in Nottingham East. Just before the general election the National Executive removed the PPC, black sections activist Sharon Atkins, on the grounds that she had called the Labour Party 'racist', and imposed local Councillor Mohammed Aslam. Michael Knowles went on to hold, by a whisker, the seat he had won in 1983.

East is a polarised marginal, ranging from leafy residential areas to inner-city Council estates, and is a marginal which should change hands fairly easily. Lady Luck must be shining, therefore, on East's Conservative MP, as the selection of a Labour PPC has been suspended pending an investigation by the national Party of alleged Trotskyist infiltration of the Party. Another Houdini act by Mr Knowles cannot entirely be ruled out.

NOTTINGHAM SOUTH

Con maj 3,234:

Con 23,921	44.7%
Lab 21,687	40.5%
SDP 7,917	14.8%

Swing required 2.1%. **Category** Labour easier win. **MP** Martin Brandon-Bravo **Lab PPC** Alan Simpson **Lib Dem PPC** Gareth Long

Nottingham South contains Pork Farms who make pies and sausages, and the Royal Ordnance who make guns. The largest employer, however, is probably the University Hospital where Prince Charles had his broken arm treated on the NHS and where an opt-out plan is currently mooted.

It is a mixed constituency. Wollaton and the university area are leafy and well-to-do. The Clifton Council estate, with over 8,000 dwellings built in the 1950s, 60s and 70s, was in its day the biggest in Europe. Right-to-buy has made enormous headway with over half of the homes sold to tenants by the end of 1990, but with record mortgage interest rates the political impact of that is now uncertain.

Alan Simpson, a race equality officer, is set for his second crack at the seat. Martin Brandon-Bravo, the oldest of the new Conservative MPs of 1983 and a well-established local figure, is reputed to have supported Michael Heseltine's challenge to Margaret Thatcher.

Labour have had their share of problems in Nottingham East, and there is the possibility of an overspill effect. Local government representation is finely balanced. Nottingham South swung to Labour by 3.8% in 1987, a better result than in the East Midlands as a whole: a similar swing this time would put Mr Simpson in Parliament.

NUNEATON

Con maj 5,655:

Con 24,630 44.9%
Lab 18,975 34.6%
SDP 10,550 19.2%
Grn 719 1.3%

Swing required 5.2%. **Category** Labour decider. **MP** Lewis Stevens **Lab PPC** Bill Olner

This once secure Labour fortress north of Coventry has been held by the rightwing Tory Lewis Stevens, since the 1983 Boundary Commission removed the former mining town of Bedworth and added three rural wards. In 1987 Labour fielded Valerie Veness, a leftwing Councillor from Islington, and she and Mr Stevens both picked up about 4% each from the 1983 SDP vote.

With the Liberal Democrats without a PPC as we go to press, there may be opportunity for local Councillor Bill Olner to squeeze the centre vote further.

SHERWOOD

Con maj 4,495:

Con 26,816 45.9%
Lab 22,321 38.2%
SDP 9,342 16.0%

Swing required 3.9%. **Category** Labour easier win. **MP** Andrew Stewart **Lab PPC** Paddy Tipping

Sherwood is made up of three parts: the northern outskirts of Nottingham; mining communities around Ollerton; and a rural, farming community to the east. It is a new constituency first contested in 1983 when, to the surprise of many, the Conservatives won.

The Notts coalfield worked through the 1984-5 Strike and became the stronghold of the breakaway Union of Democratic Mineworkers, an important factor in the increased Tory majority in 1987. Labour have been wise therefore in the choice of Paddy Tipping, a charming, well-liked County Councillor and former social worker with the Church of England Children's Society. Mr Tipping is strictly neutral on the NUM/UDM dispute.

There is no effective Liberal tradition and with Tipping a supporter of PR 'in principle', Labour may pick up former SDP voters. The ousting of Conservative farmer Andrew Stewart should be within their grasp.

STAFFORDSHIRE MID

Con maj 14,654:		
	Con 28,644	50.6%
	Lab 13,990	24.7%
	Lib 13,114	23.2%
	Oth 836	1.5%

Swing required 13%. **Category** Labour decider. **MP** Sylvia Heal (Labour) **Con PPC** Charles Prior **Lib Dem PPC** Barry Stamp

Following the suicide of Conservative MP John Heddle, the by-election in Mid Staffordshire in March 1991 gave Labour their best single result since 1935. At the time of a Labour poll zenith and the Government's poll tax nadir, Sylvia Heal snatched the seat with a majority of nearly 10,000.

Mid Staffordshire is largely a rural constituency. The only towns of any size are Rugeley, which has a coal mine and coal-fired power stations, and Lichfield, home of the Staffordshire regiment and a cathedral with three spires.

This is classic Conservative country. Without a huge Labour poll lead and without a coterie of minders from Walworth Road, Ms Heal will do extremely well to hold on.

WARWICKSHIRE NORTH

Con maj 2,829:		
	Con 25,453	45.1%
	Lab 22,624	40.1%
	SDP 8,382	14.8%

Swing required 2.5%. **Category** Labour easier win. **MP** Francis Maude **Lab PPC** Mike O'Brien

Boundary changes have made this 'rural' seat less secure for Francis Maude than his father's old Warwickshire constituency. It now includes Bedworth, the former mining town which, despite the growth of new housing estates, is solidly Labour. The rest of Warwickshire North is made up of industrial vilages around the old coalfield, and belts of commuterland.

The SDP vote fell by just over 6% in 1987, divided roughly half-and-half between Labour and the Conservatives. With any reasonable regional swing, law lecturer Mike O'Brien will win this seat at his second attempt.

WOLVERHAMPTON NORTH EAST

Con maj 204:

Con 19,857 42.1%
Lab 19,653 41.7%
Lib 7,623   16.2%

Swing required O.2%. **Category** Labour easier win. **MP** Maureen Hicks **Lab PPC** Ken Purchase

Wolverhampton North East follows York, Ayr and Dulwich in terms of smallest Conservative-over-Labour numerical majority. Former MP for over 20 years, Renee Short, had held on by only 214 votes in 1983, so it was the second photo-finish in a row in this largely working-class seat.

Mrs Maureen Hicks, a former teacher and staff manager at Marks & Spencers, has a lively local profile and will benefit from 'double incumbency' next time round. But the margin is so small that it seems likely that law lecturer Ken Purchase will capture the seat at the second attempt, and thereby reduce the already small number of female Conservative MPs.

WYRE FOREST

Con maj 7,224:

Con 25,887 47.1%
Lib 18,653 34.0%
Lab 10,365 18.9%

Swing required 7.6% **Category** Liberal Democrat target. **MP** Anthony Coombs **Lib Dem PPC** Mark Jones **Lab PPC** Ross Maden

Company director Anthony Coombs will be defending for the first time this largely residential constituency between the Midlands cities and the Welsh border.

The Liberal Democrats are very strong in local government, controlling the Wyre Forest district Council which has the same boundaries as the parliamentary seat. Success here for Mark Jones would seem to depend heavily on squeezing the Labour vote, which is generally to be found in Kidderminster and Stourport on the Severn.

Labour would require a massive swing of 14.1% to win here, and have selected the chair of the regional Party, Ross Maden, who is likely to conduct an effective campaign. The likely outcome of an improved Labour showing would be further division of the 'opposition' vote and a comfortable second term for Mr Coombs.

NORTH EAST

Yorkshire and the North East have not been notable beneficiaries of Conservative economic policies in the 1980s. The decline of traditional industries like ship-building and textiles produced high levels of unemployment, and the head-on clash with the National Union of Mineworkers in the mid-1980s left a legacy of bitterness which still lingers.

There are, of course, areas of relative economic comfort, and many northerners are proud of their efforts to develop new industries. But the region as a whole was never entirely comfortable with the hectoring south-of-England style of Mrs Thatcher, and the impression sometimes given by Tory ministers that everyone north of Nottingham ate too many chips and never exercised.

Labour has remained the dominant party here throughout the 12 years of Conservative rule, both in local authority and parliamentary terms. Yorkshire and the North East swung to Labour in 1987 by between 3% and 6%, and the swing was particularly high in South Yorkshire and Tyne & Wear.

In Yorkshire and Humberside Labour gained Glanford & Scunthorpe (defeating Richard Hickmet who went on to lose the 'safe' seat of Eastbourne in last year's by-election), Bradford North, Halifax and Dewsbury. The Tories hung on by their finger-tips in York and Batley & Spen, both of which still look ripe for Labour capture.

The swing in South Yorkshire stacked up votes in seats already held by Labour; the only remaining Tory-held seat there, Sheffield Hallam, is a Liberal Democrat target. The far North East too was already very red, and Labour's increasing share of the vote brought larger majorities in Labour seats rather than gains. But Langbaurgh, Darlington and Tynemouth are now within 'easy reach'. Labour will have high hopes too in West Yorkshire: Batley & Spen is within the 'easier win' category, and Calder Valley, Elmet and Keithley not far behind.

Liberal Democrat interest in this region centres on Sheffield Hallam, Leeds North West and Pudsey in Yorkshire; and on the two three way marginals, Stockton South up in the North East and Colne Valley in Yorkshire. Once again, part of the key to further advance for 'Paddy's army' will be encouraging Labour supporters to vote tactically.

BATLEY & SPEN

Con maj 1,362:

Con 25,512 43.5%
Lab 24,150 41.1%
SDP 8,372 14.3%
Oth 689 1.2%

Swing required 1.2%. **Category** Labour easier win. **MP** Elizabeth Peacock **Lab PPC** Eunice Durkin **Lib Dem PPC** Gordon Beever

Unusually for a northern, mainly working-class seat, Batley & Spen swung slightly to the Conservatives in 1987. Part of the reason for this was the 'double incumbency' effect benefiting Elizabeth Peacock, the Yorkshire-bred parliamentary advisor to the National Bedding Federation.

Mrs Peacock's local popularity notwithstanding, Labour's new PPC Eunice Durkin must be optimistic in a seat which, in national terms, Mr Major can afford to lose and still retain a very comfortable overall majority.

CALDER VALLEY

Con maj 6,045:

Con 25,892 43.5%
Lab 19,847 33.4%
Lib 13,361 23.1%

Swing required 5.2%. **Category** Labour decider. **MP** Donald Thompson **Lab PPC** David Chaytor

This geographically large constituency set in the lower Pennines south-west of Bradford produced in 1987 a result which roughly matched the national percentages. Labour leapfrogged the Alliance with that result, and have shown a continuing improvement in local elections.

Government poll tax regulations had one of their strangest effects on local Calderdale Council, who were poll tax capped despite having set one of the lowest figures in the country.

Labour have re-selected as PPC Councillor David Chaytor, who will hope to benefit from a favourable regional swing. He will also need to squeeze the former Alliance vote, especially as the Liberal Democrats have been slow to select a candidate. This will not be easy as the constituency, along with neighbouring Colne Valley, has something of a Liberal tradition. Conservative MP Donald Thompson is a popular local figure and looks the front-runner.

COLNE VALLEY

Con maj 1,677:	Con 20,457	36.4%
	Lib 18,780	33.4%
	Lab 16,353	29.1%
	Grn 614	1.1%

Swing required 1.5% for Liberal Democrats, 3.7% for Labour **Category** Three way marginal. **MP** Graham Riddick **Lib Dem PPC** Nigel Priestley **Lab PPC** John Harman

In the 1960s, 70s and 80s Colne Valley was regarded as a Labour/Liberal marginal. From 1966 to 1970 it was represented by Richard Wainwright for the Liberals, from 1970 to 1974 by David Clark for Labour, and after that by Mr Wainwright again.

In 1983 the Labour vote collapsed dramatically and the Conservatives found themselves in second place. In 1987, with the retirement of the popular Mr Wainwright, a 4.5% swing from the Liberals to the Conservatives was enough to give sales manager Graham Riddick victory, even though he polled not much over one third of the vote.

The 1987 contestants are set to resume battle. Both of Mr Riddick's opponents have had local profiles: solicitor Nigel Priestley as a Meltham town Councillor and a Church lay reader, and teacher John Harman as a Councillor in Kirklees district. One or the other will need to emerge as the clear 'anti-Tory' candidate in the Colne and Holme valleys which make up this three way marginal constituency.

DARLINGTON

Con maj 2,661:	Con 24,831	46.6%
	Lab 22,170	41.6%
	SDP 6,289	11.8%

Swing required 2.5%. **Category** Labour easier win. **MP** Michael Fallon **Lab PPC** Alan Milburn

Darlington was the scene in 1983 of the by-election victory for Ossie O'Brien which gave a flicker of hope to Michael Foot in the run-up to Labour's general election debacle later in that year. Mr O'Brien, having been a MP for only three months, was swept away by a Tory majority of nearly 3,500.

The 1983 victor, Michael Fallon, a former college lecturer and adviser to Lord Carrington, did well to hold on (albeit more narrowly) in 1987, in the only Durham seat flying the blue flag.

Despite the run-down and eventual closure of its famous railway works, Darlington is far from being a depressed town, and Mr Fallon, still in his 30s, will fight hard to keep his seat.

ELMET

Con Maj 5,356:

Con 25,658	46.9%
Lab 20,302	37.1%
SDP 8,755	16.0%

Swing required 4.9%. **Category** Labour decider. **MP** Spencer Batiste **Lab PPC** Colin Burgon

Elmet is a sprawling, varied constituency east of Leeds. It ranges from large Council estates on the city's fringes to the up-market commuter town of Wetherby which is skirted by the A1 and as near to the centre of York as to the centre of Leeds. It also takes in villages like Bardsey and Thorner.

MP since 1983, when the seat was first contested, Mr Spencer Batiste, solicitor and company director, is a legal adviser to the Cutlery and Silverware Association. He is also a member of Eric Hammond's EETPU and a leading figure in the Conservative Trade Unionists group.

Labour's Colin Burgon, who fought the seat unsuccessfully in 1987, is a Leeds teacher. The Liberals took over 20% of the vote in 1983 but have subsequently fallen back in what now appears a straight Conservative/Labour marginal.

KEIGHLEY

Con maj 5,606:

Con 23,903	45.8%
Lab 18,297	35.0%
Lib 10,041	19.2%

Swing required 5.4%. **Category** Labour decider. **MP** Gary Waller **Lab PPC** Tommy Flanagan **Lib Dem PPC** Richard Fogden

Based on the town of Keighley, west of Bradford, this constituency runs up to the Pennine moors, from which Emily Bronte's *Wuthering Heights* took inspiration. It also includes affluent Ilkley (by the moor of the famous bareheaded Yorkshire song).

The late 18th century brought textile mills to Keighley, imposing an industrial flavour in this beautiful part of the country. As one might expect with the social mixture that developed, the seat is a Labour/Conservative marginal that has changed hands many times since the war. It was held for Labour between 1974 and 1983 by Bob Cryer, now MP for Bradford South and leading the resistance within the Labour Party to electoral reform.

Vanquishing Mr Cryer in 1983 was Gary Waller, journalist and former MP for the now-defunct seat of Brighouse & Spenborough. Mr Waller went on to an increased majority in 1987, when (without Mr Cryer's personal vote) Labour's share fell at a time of a favourable national swing.

With the Liberals polling over 10,000 votes in 1987, a fierce battle for the centre ground appears likely.

LANGBAURGH

Con maj 2,088:	Con 26,047	41.7%
	Lab 23,959	38.4%
	Lib 12,405	19.9%

Swing required 1.7%. **Category** Labour easier win. **MP** Richard Holt **Lab PPC** Ashok Kumar **Lib Dem PPC** Peter Allen

Langbaurgh has no overall identity as a constituency. About 40% of the population live on the outskirts of Middlesbrough, the rest in a mixture of industrial towns, ex-ironstone mining villages and market towns. 'Langbaurgh' is the name of the district Council which administers Redcar and the part of the Langbaurgh parliamentary constituency which is not in Middlesbrough.

Labour are strong in local government, controlling Middlesbrough. At the time of writing they are the largest party too on Langbaurgh but are thwarted by the Conservatives who have Liberal Democrat support.

In 1983 and 1987 Labour hopes for the parliamentary seat were thwarted by Richard Holt – a forceful, if sometimes controversial, figure who was once a Councillor many miles away in High Wycombe.

With any reasonable national swing Labour should take Langbaurgh, making their PPC Ashok Kumar, reportedly the first black Councillor in the North East, the region's first black MP. Asked about his prospects, Mr Kumar wisely says he's 'not confident until the last vote is counted'.

LEEDS NORTH WEST

Con maj 5,201:	Con 22,480	43.5%
	Lib 17,279	33.5%
	Lab 11,210	21.7%
	Grn 663	1.3%

Swing required 5%. **Category** Liberal Democrat target. **MP** Keith Hampson **Lib Dem PPC** Barbara Pearce **Lab PPC** Sue Egan

Leeds North West is a comfortable residential part of the city, including Headingly cricket ground, scene of many epic England vs Australia and Yorkshire vs Lancashire engagements.

MP since 1983 is Keith Hampson, who has been parliamentary private secretary to both Tom King and Michael Heseltine. As a former university lecturer (in

American history), and a consultant to the university teachers' trade union, the AUT, his style and tone are well suited to this generally leafy constituency.

The Liberals bucked the national trend by achieving a 3.8% swing from the Tories in 1987, with Labour static in third place.

PUDSEY

Con maj 6,436:

Con	25,457	45.5%
Lib	19,021	34.0%
Lab	11,461	20.5%

Swing required 5.8%. **Category** Liberal Democrat target. **MP** Sir Giles Shaw **Lab PPC** Arthur Giles

Pudsey constituency is a conglomerate of towns just to the west of Leeds, including Pudsey itself. It is within easy commuting distance of Leeds and therefore an attractive bet for many of the city's better-off employees.

Sir Giles, marketing director at Rowntree Mackintosh before his election in 1974, has held a variety of junior ministerial posts – Northern Ireland, Environment, Energy, the Home Office and Trade and Industry. In the following general elections Sir Giles has consistently polled around 45% of the vote, with the Liberals seemingly unable to squeeze the Labour vote. With only the Labour Party having selected a PPC as we go to press, Sir Giles must be strong favourite to win another term.

SHEFFIELD HALLAM

Con maj 7,637:

Con	25,649	46.3%
Lib	18,012	32.5%
Lab	11,290	20.4%
Grn	459	0.8%

Swing required 6.9%. **Category** Liberal Democrat target. **MP** Irvine Patnick **Lib Dem PPC** Peter Gold **Lab PPC** Veronica Hardstaff

Hallam is the only one of the six Sheffield seats which is held by the Conservatives. Custodian of the blue banner is Irvine Patnick, a well-known city figure who was both county and city Councillor before becoming a MP in 1987.

The constituency, which runs from the south-west outskirts of the city nearly as far as the Peak District contains a high proportion of professionals. Given the proximity of its north-easterly parts to the university (in the Sheffield Central seat), there are also a large number of students.

Liberal Democrat PPC Peter Gold, a lecturer in Spanish studies, has played a national role in the formation of Party foreign policy. Mr Gold increased the centre share of the vote in 1987, and there is a significant Labour vote for him to squeeze.

STOCKTON SOUTH

Con maj 774:

Con 20,833 35.0%
SDP 20,059 33.7%
Lab 18,600 31.3%

Swing required 0.7% for Liberal Democrats, 1.9% for Labour.
Category Three way marginal. **MP** Tim Devlin **Lib Dem PPC** Ian Wrigglesworth **Lab PPC** John Scott

Britain's first railway from Stockton to Darlington saw the early runs of George Stephenson's 'rocket'. Ian Wrigglesworth, the MP for Thornaby from February 1974, jumped the Labour train in March 1981 when the SDP was gathering steam. He held on to the new seat of Stockton South in 1983 under his new livery but was derailed in a classic three way encounter in 1987.

The other passenger who narrowly missed the train that year was John Scott, a higher education tutor who first became a borough Councillor in 1960. Catching his connection for Westminster was Tim Devlin, a sprightly 27 years old at the time. All three gentlemen are ready again, waiting for station-master John Major to blow the whistle.

Predictions in seats like this are even less reliable than British Rail time-tables. Mr Devlin's 'double incumbency' advantage would be easily outweighed by any reasonable North East swing to Labour, but Mr Wrigglesworth is still well-known locally and perhaps an attractive alternative for disillusioned Tories in this more well-to-do end of town. Any tactical voters in the signal box can be excused for being uncertain as to which lever to pull.

TYNEMOUTH

Con maj 2,583:

Con 25,113 43.2%
Lab 22,530 38.8%
Lib 10,446 18.0%

Swing required 2.2%. **Category** Labour easier win. **MP** Neville Trotter **Lab PPC** Paddy Cosgrove **Lib Dem PPC** Philip Selby

Tynemouth is, unsurprisingly, to be found where the river Tyne meets the North Sea, taking in the town of Tynemouth itself and a line of seaside resorts like Whitley Bay. It is the only Conservative-held seat in the Labour stronghold of Tyne & Wear.

The banks of the Tyne were once a series of thriving shipyards. The North East's role as a major shipbuilder has been in steady decline since at least the Great War, but Tyneside's character remains set. Tynemouth is solidly working-class and solidly Labour.

Support for Neville Trotter has come mainly from further north. The seaside resorts tend to the Conservatives, and the territory inland is almost suburban. That said, Labour increased its share of the vote in the constituency from 31% in 1983 to nearly 39% in 1987. There is no Liberal tradition here worth speaking of, and for barrister Paddy Cosgrove, now in his early 40s, it looks as if it may be 'third time lucky' in the Tynemouth constituency.

YORK

Con maj 147:

Con	25,880	41.6%
Lab	25,773	41.4%
SDP	9,898	15.9%
Grn	637	1.0%

Swing required 0.1%. **Category** Labour easier win. **MP** Conal Gregory **Lab PPC** Hugh Bayley **Lib Dem PPC** Karen Anderson

York has the smallest majority of any Conservative-held seat in Britain. A university town, it is famous for Rowntree chocolate, its cathedral and railway works.

Its MP since 1983, Conal Gregory, is a colourful figure. In 1985, he arranged a visit to the House of Commons for Miss World contestants. When he claimed that British beauty queens were short on intelligence, the *Daily Mail* kindly arranged a general-knowledge quiz with Miss UK Mandy Shires. Mr Gregory scored 10 out of 30, against Ms Squires's 13 (Mr Gregory thought the capital of Saudi Arabia was Addis Ababa; Ms Squires knew it was Riyadh). *Tatler* magazine awarded him a prize for being 'stupidly caught out as an ignoramus'.

Mr Gregory went on to further distinction by arranging a photo-call at a weed-ridden roundabout to publicise the need to privatise the Council's Park Department. Unfortunately he chose the only roundabout whose upkeep was already the responsibility of a private company.

Labour's prospective candidate Hugh Bayley is sober in comparison. A health economist and member of the Labour Campaign for Electoral Reform, he promotes himself as a sound prospect for a good constituency MP. Even the city's gentrification symbolised by Bishop's Wharf is unlikely to stop Mr Bayley taking up that challenge.

NORTH WEST

The simple image of the blue South and the red North is confounded by the realities of the North West. There are still a large number of Conservative seats which survived the 1987 regional swing of about 3.5% to Labour – ten, for example, in Greater Manchester as against Labour's 19. And despite a massive swing to Labour on Merseyside in 1987, electoral geography meant that the Tories lost only one seat, Southport, and that to the Liberal Ronnie Fearn.

The North West is socially diverse, ranging from the industrial landscape of Liverpool and Ellesmere Port to Ribble Valley, one of the most agricultural constituencies in the country. It contains a large number of marginal seats of all varieties: seats like Bolton North East, Hyndburn and Wallasey where the Conservatives have tiny majorities over Labour; the two Blackpool constituencies whose capture could signal an overall Labour majority; and Chester, where Labour have never had an MP but are now hopeful.

Liberal Democrat interest in the region is focused on Hazel Grove where the Liberal Democrats have one of their best chances of a parliamentary gain in the country; Congleton which is very much a Liberal Democrat long-shot; Littleborough & Saddleworth, held by Geoffrey Dickens, but where either Labour or the Liberal Democrats could win; and Liverpool Mossley Hill where Labour hope to overcome the Liberal Democrats' David Alton.

The North West contains areas of high unemployment and social decay. Liverpool, a city of massive poverty, has seen both rioting and the near-collapse of local government through the conflict of a Militant/Labour Council and a Government committed to free enterprise and the high pound. The textile towns of Lancashire have also become the home of high unemployment and low wages, undermining the long tradition of local working-class Toryism which held up Labour's advance in 1987 in Hyndburn, Bury North and Bolton North East.

It seems likely that any swing away from the Government will be larger in the North West than in the country as a whole; and (given the area's electoral geography) this swing will be translated into the loss of Conservative-held seats. This makes the North West of enormous importance to the outcome of the general election.

BARROW & FURNESS

Con maj 3,927:   Con 25,431 46.5%
                        Lab 21,504 39.3%
                        SDP 7,999 14.2%

Swing required 3.6%. **Category** Labour easier win. **MP** Cecil Franks **Lab PPC** John Hutton **Lib Dem PPC** Clive Crane

Barrow is known for building nuclear submarines. Sitting at the end of the Furness peninsula, it is the most isolated large town in England. The constituency also includes a large part of South Lakeland as its rural hinterland.

As a centre of the nuclear weapons industry, it was inevitable that Barrow should turn strongly against Labour in the 1983 election, despite being overwhelmingly a working class town. Labour made up a little ground in 1987, and its progress this time will be a test of Neil Kinnock's success in defusing the nuclear defence issue. With the peace dividend already bringing cut-backs and lay offs in the Vickers submarine yards, the voters of Barrow could well decide that Labour is now more likely to represent their best interests.

John Hutton fought Penrith and the Borders in 1987; originally a southerner he lives across the Pennines in Hexham. But he is as much a local man as Cecil Franks, who comes from Manchester. He has a good chance of spending some of his time in Westminster after the election.

BLACKPOOL NORTH

Con maj 7,321:   Con 20,680 48.0%
                        Lab 13,359 31.0%
                        Lib 9,032   21.0%

Swing required 8.5%. **Category** Labour decider. **MP** Norman Miscampbell (retiring) **Con PPC** Harold Elletson **Lab PPC** Eric Kirton

Labour are optimistic about their chances in both Blackpool seats, given that both sitting MPs are retiring. The home of the seaside landlady and of the famous illuminations, Blackpool may not seem very promising territory for socialism, but local unemployment is as high as 25% in some wards.

Labour has chosen Eric Kirton as PPC. He fought the seat in 1987 but was selected only three months before the general election. Mr Kirton is the backroom agent behind Labour's local government election campaign, and is hoping that a good showing in the 1991 Council elections will transfer into parliamentary support. This may be too optimistic given the increasing divergence between the way people vote locally and nationally.

Blackpool's Liberal Democrats are still chewing over the old chestnut about what their name should be, and are without a PPC at time of going to press. Labour must hope to poach from their following.

Mr Kirton became a borough Councillor in 1971 and a County Councillor in 1981, and so believes that fate shines on him when the year ends in a '1'. Since the capture of Blackpool North might indicate a Labour majority Government, Mr Major might like to ponder this when choosing the date of the general election.

BLACKPOOL SOUTH

Con maj 6,744:

Con	20,312	48.0%
Lab	13,568	32.1%
Lib	8,405	19.9%

Swing required 8%. **Category** Labour decider. **MP** Sir Peter Blaker (retiring) **Con PPC** Nicholas Hawkins **Lab PPC** Gordon Marsden

Unlike the North seat, the Tories here have selected a local candidate, Nicholas Hawkins. Labour plan to field Gordon Marsden, who is from the other Party Conference venue, Brighton, but who – with his good looks and polished approach – is very much a 'New Model Party' candidate.

The seat is very similar socially and politically to Blackpool North. Although the swing required here is less, Labour did better in the North in the 1989 County elections (where they out-polled the Tories) than in the South (where they did not).

BOLTON NORTH EAST

Con maj 813:

Con	20,742	44.4%
Lab	19,929	42.6%
SDP	6,060	13.0%

Swing required 0.9%. **Category** Labour easier win. **MP** Peter Thurnham **Lab PPC** David Crausby **Lib Dem PPC** Brian Dunning

Bolton North East is a middle-of-the-road sort of constituency – about average for the country in social composition, reasonably prosperous, a mixture of urban and suburban wards. It also has one of the smallest Conservative majorities. Peter Thurnham hung on last time against a smaller swing than the regional average.

David Crausby is a long-time activist in the Engineering Workers' Union and a supporter of Bury football club. Mr Crausby has a much better chance of reaching Westminster than Bury have of reaching Wembley.

BOLTON WEST

Con maj 4,593:

Con 24,779 44.3%
Lab 20,186 36.1%
SDP 10,936 19.6%

Swing required 3.9%. **Category** Labour easier win. **MP** Tom Sackville **Lab PPC** Cliff Morris **Lib Dem PPC** Barbara Ronson

In the far-off days when Liberals were much readier to ally with Tories than they are now, Bolton was divided between the two parties. The Tories gave the Liberals a free run in Bolton West, and the Liberals stood down in Bolton East. The pact came to an end in 1964, and the Liberals and their successors are now just fractionally stronger in Bolton West than in the surrounding constituencies.

So although this will basically be a straight fight between Tory and Labour in Bolton West, the fight could go to the candidate who eats into the former Alliance vote most successfully. Despite having represented the seat since 1983, old-Etonian Tom Sackville is still only 40, able and energetic. Labour will do well to take the seat, which includes a high proportion of owner-occupiers and the best residential areas in Bolton.

BURY NORTH

Con maj 6,929:

Con 28,097 50.1%
Lab 21,168 37.8%
Lib 6,804 12.1%

Swing required 6.2%. **Category** Labour decider. **MP** Alistair Burt **Lab PPC** Jim Dobbin

Very unusually for Lancashire, and for the North West, Bury North swung to the Conservatives in 1987. Worryingly for Labour, this may have been due in part to a growing prosperity in the birthplace of Sir Robert Peel.

However, Bury South is socially not very different and swung to Labour at the same time. And in 1983 Labour held its ground in North, despite its lowest share of the national vote since 1918. Part of the explanation is the 'double incumbency' enjoyed by Alistair Burt, and part that the seat was no longer contested by the very popular former Labour MP Frank White.

Voters here are historically volatile – Labour did not win Bury in the landslide of 1945 – and Scot Jim Dobbin will have a lot of hard persuading to do.

BURY SOUTH

Con maj 2,679:

Con 23,878 46.1%
Lab 21,199 40.9%
SDP 6,722 13.1%

Swing required 2.6%. **Category** Labour easier win. **MP** David Sumberg **Lab PPC** Hazel Blears **Lib Dem PPC** Adrian Cruden

As a consultant to the Northern Independent Bookmakers' Association, David Sumberg no doubt commands good advice on his chances of being re-elected this time. Bury South is the sort of seat Labour ought to win. Although it includes some desirable residential areas, such as Prestwich, it is not going up in the world any more; the newer generation commuters are tending to move further out to more picturesque towns.

David Sumberg, junior minister, solicitor and former member of Manchester City Council, will be opposed by Hazel Blears, another solicitor, who works for Manchester. Still only 35, she fought the solidly Tory seat of Tatton in Cheshire last time and could provide some useful extra expertise for Labour's small band of women in Parliament.

CHESTER CITY

Con maj 4,855:

Con 23,582 44.9%
Lab 18,727 35.6%
Lib 10,262 19.5%

Swing required 4.7%. **Category** Labour easier win. **MP** Peter Morrison (retiring) **Con PPC** Gyles Brandreth **Lab PPC** David Robinson **Lib Dem PPC** Gordon Smith

At first glance this originally Roman city appears an unlikely bet for Labour, but most of the North West of England moved leftwards in 1987 and may move still further.

Chester-born-and-bred local teacher David Robinson was the beneficiary then (winning the same 35% as in 1979) and has been re-selected as PPC. The Liberal/Alliance candidate of 1987, Andrew Stunell, has moved on to greener pastures at Hazel Grove.

Mr Robinson will hope to squeeze the centre vote in pursuit of the Conservative PPC Gyles Brandreth, joke book author and television personality. (The former deputy Chairman at Conservative Central Office, Peter Morrison, is retiring.) Chester has never had a Labour MP, but the 1987 result means that it is on the border of the 'Labour easier win'/'Labour decider' categories. For Mr Kinnock, a crucial seat in a crucial region.

CHORLEY

Con maj 8,057:		
	Con 29,015	48.0%
	Lab 20,958	34.7%
	Lib 9,706	16.1%
	Grn 714	1.2%

Swing required 6.7%. **Category** Labour decider. **MP** Denshaw Dover **Lab PPC** Ray McManus **Lib Dem PPC** Janet Ross-Mills

Chorley has been held by the Conservatives when Edward Heath and Margaret Thatcher (plus John Major) have been Prime Minister. It was Labour from 1945 to 1970 and again during the Wilson/Callaghan governments of 1974-9. Boundary changes in the early 1980s tilted the seat slightly rightwards.

Civil engineer Den Dover, MP now for 12 years, achieved a majority of over 10,000 in 1983, and even with a 2.2% swing to Labour in 1987 he held on very comfortably.

Chorley town is industrial and tends to Labour, especially in local elections. To the north, Euxton and Clayton-le-Woods incline to the Conservatives. Labour's Ray McManus, in his late 40s, and a Transport & General Workers' Union official from Skelmersdale, will have to counter a friendly prejudice against 'Scousers' in the sleepier, more rural parts of the constituency!

CONGLETON

Con maj 7,969:		
	Con 26,513	48.3%
	Lib 18,544	33.8%
	Lab 9,810	17.9%

Swing required 7.3%. **Category** Liberal Democrat target. **MP** Ann Winterton **Lib Dem PPC** Iain Brodie-Brown **Lab PPC** Matt Finagan

Congleton constituency is made up of small towns and villages in the south east of Cheshire, including Congleton itself. Local Councillor Iain Brodie-Brown is set for his second crack at a seat where the Liberals have made advances at each of the last three general elections, though in 1987 this was largely at the expense of Labour, whose vote fell.

The Liberal Democrats are strong in local government. Cross-party agreement with Labour on a hung Cheshire County Council became a model for others to follow. In the 1990 local elections Labour and the Liberal Democrats were neck-and-neck with the Tories trailing in third place.

Translating such good local performance into parliamentary success may not be easy for the Liberal Democrats, here as elsewhere. The sitting MP, Ann Winterton, whose husband represents neighbouring Macclesfield, has a high local profile.

CROSBY

Con maj 6,853:

Con 30,842 46.1%
SDP 23,989 35.9%
Lab 11,992 17.9%

Swing required 5.1%. **Category** Liberal Democrat target. **MP** Malcolm Thornton **Lib Dem PPC** Flo Clucas

This belt of middle-class commuterland was the scene of a famous by-election triumph for the SDP back in 1981, but the victor Shirley Williams could not hold on in 1983 even though the Alliance won over a quarter of the vote at national level.

Malcolm Thornton doubled his majority in 1987, this time over Scott Donovan, as Ms Williams had departed to fight Cambridge (unsuccessfully). The seat remains theoretically within reach, although much past activity in the seat was SDP- rather than Liberal-generated.

Local Liberal Democrats have selected a campaigner of many years' experience, Liverpool Councillor Flo Clucas. She may hope that success in the neighbouring (and socially similar) constituency of Southport, snatched by Ronnie Fearn in 1987, will rub off here.

DAVYHULME

Con maj 8,199:

Con 23,633 46.6%
Lab 15,434 30.4%
Lib 11,637 23.0%

Swing required 8.1%. **Category** Labour decider. **MP** Winston Churchill **Lab PPC** Barry Brotherton **Lib Dem PPC** Jacqueline Pearcey

Davyhulme is made up of well-to-do suburbs south-west of Manchester, with the sole exception of industrial workers from the ICI chemical plant at Carrington. Labour was closer to third than first in 1987 and describing this seat as marginal gives a clear idea of the size of the task facing Labour if it is to win an overall parliamentary majority. This task may not be made easier by the resonance of the name Winston Churchill, which commands international recognition on the same sort of scale as Bobby Charlton. Mr Churchill the grandson is respected locally and has made an effective television communicator.

Labour and Tories are side-by-side in terms of votes in local elections, and Trafford Council made news in the first year of the poll tax by fixing one of the lowest of all the metropolitan districts. Labour's Barry Brotherton, leader of Trafford Labour group hopes to squeeze the third place former Alliance vote, particularly as the Liberal Democrats have not selected a candidate at time of press and are fielding very few candidates in local elections.

ELLESMERE PORT & NESTON

Con maj 1,853:		
	Con 25,664	44.4%
	Lab 23,811	41.2%
	SDP 8,143	14.1%
	Oth 185	0.3%

Swing required 1.6%. **Category** Labour easier win. **MP** Michael Woodcock **Lab PPC** Andrew Miller **Lib Dem PPC** Elizabeth Mould

Ellesmere Port was originally the outlet to the sea for the canal built in the early 19th century for the Shropshire market town of Ellesmere which is 30 miles inland. Linked also to the Manchester Ship Canal, the rapid growth of Ellesmere Port as an industrial town swallowed up the village of Whitby, and it now contains docks, chemical refineries and a Vauxhall car plant. Its population of around 45,000 comprises more than half the electorate.

The constituency runs across from the Mersey estuary to the Dee estuary, on which stand Neston, originally a mining village (the mine shut in 1926), and Parkgate, once famed for its oysters but now silted up. Whilst Ellesmere is solidly Labour, Neston and Parkgate are two pretty sandstone villages with new estates with romantic names and Conservative-inclined voters.

Further inland there is a scattering of smaller towns and villages with a population that commutes to both Chester and Liverpool. The constituency also includes the uranium enrichment plant at Capenhurst.

After a poor result in 1983, Labour stormed back in 1987 with a 5% swing. Their PPC this time round, Andrew Miller, is an official with the Managerial, Scientific and Finance (MSF) trade union, who moved to the area to work in 1977

This is a complex, mixed constituency without a natural focus, but – with a favourable trend in this part of the country – should slip into Labour's grasp.

HAZEL GROVE

Con maj 1,840:		
	Con 24,396	45.5%
	Lib 22,556	42.0%
	Lab 6,354	11.8%
	Grn 346	0.6%

Swing required 2.8%. **Category** Liberal Democrat target. **MP** Sir Tom Arnold **Lib Dem PPC** Andrew Stunell **Lab PPC** Gordon McAlister

Hazel Grove is a slice of suburban England bordering the Peak National Park. Residents, many of whom commute to Manchester and Stockport, mix concern for their environment with concern for their prosperity.

The seat is a classic Conservative/Liberal marginal. It was held briefly by Liberal Michael Winstanley between February and October 1974 when it was captured by Tom Arnold. Arnold won comfortably in 1979, but in both 1983 and 1987 his majority was around 2,000.

The NHS and the poll tax have been contentious local issues. Manchester's Christie hospital, specialising in cancer care, is set to 'opt out', and there have been ward closures at Stepping Hill, just outside the constituency.

Hazel Grove is part of Stockport borough which set a poll tax of £450. As the Council has a minority Liberal Democrat administration, the local Conservatives have attempted to deflect blame for the tax away from the Government. Wisely so perhaps, for even at a low point in national fortunes in May 1990, the Liberal Democrats won 14 out of 18 Council seats in the constituency.

Liberal Democrat prospective candidate, Andrew Stunell, is national secretary of the Association of Liberal Democrat Councillors. As (in his own words) 'a full-time politician by a factor of two' he is likely to conduct a canny campaign. The Labour vote is concentrated in Great Moor ward on the outskirts of Stockport itself, and squeezing it will be important for Mr Stunell.

Tom Arnold, a popular and charismatic MP knighted in 1990, will offer formidable resistance. An interesting contest is in prospect.

HIGH PEAK

Con maj 9,516:

Con	25,715	45.7%
Lab	16,199	28.8%
SDP	14,389	25.6%

Swing required 8%. **Category** Labour decider. **MP** Christopher Hawkins (retiring) **Con PPC** Charles Hendry **Lab PPC** Tom Levitt **Lib Dem PPC** Simon Molloy

Much of the area of this large constituency between Manchester and Sheffield is taken up with the wild moorlands of Kinder Scout, but the voters live in small towns in the valleys. Buxton has succeeded in recovering some of its former glory as a spa town, and places like Glossop, Hayfield and rambler-centre Chapel-en-le-Frith are increasingly commuter villages for Manchester.

David Marquand, author of 'The Meaning of Major' (chapter 2), fought High Peak for the SDP in 1983, and came second to Christopher Hawkins. Labour overtook the Alliance in 1987, but with a majority over 16%, spreading gentrification, and both his opponents new to the role, Mr Hawkins must have a good chance of winning again this time. Teacher Tom Levitt has a better chance here than he had in Stroud in the last election, but he needs a far greater swing than the 1.7% his Party achieved here in 1987.

HYNDBURN

Con maj 2,220:	Con 21,606	44.4%
	Lab 19,386	39.8%
	SDP 7,423	15.2%
	Grn 297	0.6%

Swing required 2.3%. **Category** Labour easier win. **MP** Kenneth Hargreaves **Lab PPC** Greg Pope

Hyndburn had the second smallest Tory majority after the 1983 election, yet far from losing it in 1987, Kenneth Hargreaves succeeded in increasing his majority by more than 2,000. The 'double incumbency' effect must have helped as he erased the memory of his predecessor Arthur Davidson who held the former Accrington seat from 1966 to 1983. But the fact that the Labour candidate, Keva Coombes, was also leader of strife-torn Liverpool Council must have been a factor.

The textile workers who once set the tone for Accrington and the other small towns of Hyndburn have now almost disappeared. Their successors may be open to a more forward-looking Labour appeal, but they are eager to distance themselves from the inner-city workerism which Liverpool has come to symbolise. Labour has a new candidate, but observers feel it may still be mired with the same political errors.

LANCASHIRE WEST

Con maj 1,353:	Con 26,500	43.7%
	Lab 25,147	41.5%
	SDP 8,972	14.8%

Swing required 1.1%. **Category** Labour easier win. **MP** Kenneth Hind **Lab PPC** Colin Pickthall **Lib Dem PPC** Bob Jermyn

Lancashire West is inland from Southport and Crosby. It includes Skelmersdale, a new town with Liverpool overspill and an unemployment black spot; Ormskirk, a royalist stronghold in the civil war, and now inclined to the Conservatives; and a collection of smaller rural towns and villages.

Barrister and rugby fan Kenneth Hind won the seat when it was first contested in 1983, but there was a large swing of 5.1% to Labour in 1987. Labour's Colin Picknall, literature lecturer and cricket fan, is set for his second crack at the seat and must be very optimistic about bowling Mr Hind out.

LANCASTER

Con maj 6,453:		
	Con 21,142	46.7%
	Lab 14,689	32.4%
	Lib 9,003	19.9%
	Grn 473	1.0%

Swing required 7.7%. **Category** Labour decider. **MP** Dame Elaine Kellett-Bowman **Lab PPC** Ruth Henig

When Jeffrey Archer recently addressed Lancaster Conservatives, he said that whichever party wins the constituency will be the Government. This is not necessarily true: on the list of Labour targets by size of Tory majority, the seat is 78th, and if Labour won all 78 it would be the largest party.

Lancaster is an old town. The castle still contains the Norman keep built in the twelfth century; Bonnie Prince Charlie stayed here in 1745, reputedly in the house that is now the Conservative club! But away from the Georgian streets in the centre, there are Labour-inclined areas, although their influence on the parliamentary result has to be set off against the constituency's surrounding rural areas.

Dame Kellett-Bowman has enormous campaigning experience: she has contested 11 parliamentary elections, the last seven successfully and in Lancaster. She also managed to find time to sit in the European Parliament from 1975 to 1984. (Her husband Peter was MEP for Lancashire East until 1984.) A former barrister, farmer and social worker, now in her late 60s, she still has great energy and a strong local following.

Political couples are, in fact, not unusual here, as Labour's PPC Ruth Henig is the wife of the only Labour MP Lancaster has ever had – Stanley Henig, who held the seat from 1966 to 1970. Mr Henig now leads the Labour group on the hung City Council, on which Labour and the Tories are fairly evenly matched (although Labour hold a majority of the seats in the parliamentary constituency).

Labour managed a 5.6% swing here in 1987, so this could be a very interesting seat to watch.

LITTLEBOROUGH & SADDLEWORTH

Con maj 6,202:		
	Con 22,027	43.1%
	Lib 15,825	30.9%
	Lab 13,229	26.0%

Swing required 6.1% for Liberal Democrats, 8.6% for Labour. **Category** Three way marginal. **MP** Geoffrey Dickens **Lib Dem PPC** Chris Davies

The bitter contention between Liberal and Labour in many Pennine constituencies is one of the main factors which has helped Geoffrey Dickens hold onto this seat with only 43% of the vote, despite his attempts to qualify as Westminster's licensed buffoon. (To be fair he has kept a lower profile lately than he had in the 1983-7 Parliament.)

Despite a strong challenge from Labour, Liberal Chris Davies managed to maintain the Alliance's share of the vote in 1987. A PR consultant and former chair of Liverpool housing committee, Davies is a formidable campaigner. Even so, and notwithstanding Geoffrey Dickens' failings, it must be long odds against a Liberal Democrat victory here next time. On the other hand, they won six out of eight local Council seats in May 1990.

PENDLE

Con maj 2,639:

Con 21,009 40.4%
Lab 18,370 35.3%
Lib 12,662 24.3%

Swing required 2.6%. **Category** Labour easier win. **MP** John Lee **Lab PPC** Gordon Prentice

The persistent failure of the Liberals to overtake Labour as the main challenger to the Tories in Pendle must be a source of continuing frustration to Tony Greaves, the guru of community politics, who numbers membership of Pendle Council among his many other activities. But offering a left-wing alternative to Labour has proved to have a limited appeal to local voters.

Greaves' ally and Liberal theoretician, Gordon Lishman, managed to increase the Alliance vote fractionally in 1987, but it remained a long way behind the Labour score. As of March 1991, the Liberal Democrats had still not selected a candidate. In a seat which they have fought so hard in the past, inspired by Greaves the super-activist, cynics find it hard to believe this is mere slackness.

Whatever the reason, this increasingly looks a seat where Labour should be able to achieve an above average swing in their favour. The lucid, likeable Scot Gordon Prentice has a welter of political experience, both in the backroom at Labour's Walworth Road as a local government researcher, and in the public eye as a former Leader of Hammersmith & Fulham Council in west London. Mr Prentice is hoping to form a husband-and-wife team with his wife Bridget who is standing in Lewisham East.

John Lee went on record years ago with his concerns about the effect of the poll tax on the low-rated terraces of Pendle, and as Nigel Lawson remarked 'there is no painless way out of this'. The Major U-turn is bound to leave some collateral damage in its wake.

RIBBLE VALLEY

Con maj 19,528:	Con 30,186	60.9%
	SDP 10,608	21.4%
	Lab 8,781	17.7%

Swing required 19.8%. **Category** Liberal Democrat target. **MP** Mike Carr (Liberal Democrat) **Con PPC** Nigel Evans **Lab PPC** Josie Farrington

Ribble Valley, respresented from 1979 to 1990 by former Home Secretary David Waddington until his move to the Lords, was the scene of a dramatic Liberal Democrat by-election victory in March 1991. The constituency is set in rural Lancashire, with its largest town Clitheroe having a population of no more than 14,000.

Ribble Valley had been the 13th safest Conservative seat in the country, and its loss led rapidly to the Government's about-turn on the poll tax. However, an exit poll suggested that in a general election on the same day a Conservative MP would have been elected.

Mike Carr's victory was assisted by a flood of helpers brought in from elsewhere, and, unlike Eastbourne (the scene of another recent Liberal Democrat by-election success), there is no strong Liberal presence on the Council and the local Party is weak. Mr Carr has only a matter of weeks or months to use the advantages of incumbency to make his mark.

ROSSENDALE & DARWEN

Con maj 4,982:	Con 28,056	46.6%
	Lab 23,074	38.3%
	Lib 9,097	15.1%

Swing required 4.2%. **Category** Labour easier win. **MP** David Trippier **Lab PPC** Janet Anderson **Lib Dem PPC** Kevin Connor

This is a constituency of old mill towns: Haslingden, Rawtenstall, Stacksteads and Bacup, strung out along a narrow valley in the uplands of the Rossendale Forest, and linked with Darwen, across the hills to the west, to make up the numbers. Commuters and new industry are moving into the towns of picturesque terraces.

David Trippier, once a stockbroker and now a junior minister, faces experienced opposition. Janet Anderson, who works at Labour Party headquarters in London, fought the seat in 1987 and gained a good 3.5% swing in her favour. She has good local connections too, as a former assistant to two of Blackburn's best-known MPs, Jack Straw and Barbara Castle. Meanwhile the Liberal Democrats, though they do have pockets of local strength, were late in choosing a PPC.

SOUTH RIBBLE

Con maj 8,430:		
	Con 28,133	47.2%
	Lab 19,703	33.1%
	Lib 11,746	19.7%

Swing required 7.5%. **Category** Labour decider. **MP** Robert Atkins **Lab PPC** Geoffrey Smith

With recent industrial and housing developments, parts of South Ribble have a 'new town' feel, particularly Leyland and Walton (and as one might guess from the name, there is a massive vehicle plant at Leyland). Whilst not as rural as the neighbouring Ribble Valley of by-election fame, the constituency has a smattering of small towns and villages.

Labour were very late in selecting a PPC, former RAF Wing Commander Geoffrey Smith, which will increase their difficulties in confronting Robert Atkins, a good, moderate constituency MP who has held government office.

STOCKPORT

Con maj 2,853:		
	Con 19,410	41.4%
	Lab 16,557	35.3%
	SDP 10,365	22.1%

Swing required 3.1%. **Category** Labour easier win. **MP** Anthony Favell **Lab PPC** Ann Coffey

This was one of the constituencies where a defection to the SDP led to a big majority for the Conservatives in 1983. Shirley Haines made up a lot of lost ground in 1987, leaving social worker Ann Coffey in striking distance of victory next time. Anthony Favell has been MP since 1983 and also has a strong interest in social services – he was parliamentary private secretary to John Major when the latter was Minister for Social Security and the Disabled.

Stockport is as much a mix of the old and new North West as anywhere. Areas like Heaton Mersey are prosperous commuter suburbs for Manchester and the new industries springing up on its fringes. The town itself retains something of its former 'satanic mills' atmosphere, not least because of the magnificent railway viaduct which marches across the centre.

WALLASEY

Con maj 279:		
	Con 22,791	42.5%
	Lab 22,512	41.9%
	SDP 8,363	15.6%

Swing required 0.3%. **Category** Labour easier win. **MP** Lynda Chalker

Wallasey is the seat of Lynda Chalker, one of the women John Major did not appoint to his cabinet. With a wafer-thin majority and a continuing tide running in Labour's favour round Merseyside, she must be the prominent Tory most likely to lose a seat this time.

This would be the first time Wallasey has gone Labour – the Tories held it even in 1945. But socio-economic decline has been nibbling away at the standing of the commuter suburbs, and New Brighton, like other seaside resorts, has shown a shift to the left as it has fallen on hard times.

The selection process for a Labour PPC is currently awaiting the outcome of a wider enquiry by the Walworth Road HQ into alleged Trotskyist infiltration in the Wirral. Wallasey is nextdoor to Birkenhead where there has been a long running, and as yet unresolved, battle over the attempt to de-select Frank Field MP. Depending on the timing of the general election, this may end with the imposition of a candidate; how that might affect the way Wallasey people vote remains to be seen.

WARRINGTON SOUTH

Con maj 3,609:		
	Con 24,809	42.0%
	Lab 21,200	35.9%
	Lib 13,112	22.2%

Swing required 3.1%. **Category** Labour easier win. **MP** Christopher Butler **Lab PPC** Mike Hall **Lib Dem PPC** Peter Walker

Misleadingly named, Warrington South has chosen Tory MPs because it is dominated by a stretch of middle-class Cheshire rather than the industrial town of Warrington. It has little overlap with the Warrington seat which Roy Jenkins nearly won from Labour in the SDP's first by-election, back in 1981.

Despite losing the Brecon & Radnor by-election to Liberal Richard Livsey in 1985, Chris Butler, market resarcher and journalist, was forgiven soon enough to slide into Warrington South in succession to Mark Carlisle, once Tory Secretary of State for Education and Science. Labour should be able to defeat him this time.

SCOTLAND

There is a lot of talk and some evidence that the Major premiership might mean another chance for the Tory party in Scotland. But in spite of some encouraging local results and the good polling figures that followed Thatcher's exit and the Gulf War, things are far from rosy for the Conservatives. It would be wrong to think that the only reason for the Tory slump was an unpopular leader.

Last general election they lost half their seats – 21 down to ten and it is easily conceivable that this ten will be halved again. All ten are marginal, and six would be lost on a swing of 5% or less to the second-placed party.

Labour had a total net gain of 20 seats in the 1987 general election, and nine were in Scotland. Both the SNP and the Alliance made a net gain of one north of the border.

One of the reasons for the rout was an impressive display of tactical voting against the Tories, particularly between Nationalist and Alliance supporters. If there is a repeat of this the Conservative Member of Parliament may need 'protected species' status in Scotland.

Complacency should not be a problem for the Conservatives this election. In fact, confidence will be in short supply anywhere outside Dumfries or Eastwood. As for the other parties, Labour are in confident mood and expect to improve on the 48 seats they already hold in Scotland. The Liberal Democrats have lost some momentum but having set their sights on two Tory constituencies they will go about trying to win them in dogged fashion.

At worst the SNP expect a couple of high-profile victories. However, if they can convince voters before the election that Labour will be unable to form a Government then the Nationalists can expect much more. Yet another Tory win and the shelving of the Scottish Constitutional Convention will bring a massive boost in SNP membership. Seat by seat, Labour look like the best bet in Ayr and Stirling, and should run Malcolm Rifkind close in Edinburgh Pentlands. The SNP sense victory in Perth & Kinross, Tayside North and most of all in Galloway, where they are hoping to scalp Scottish Secretary Ian Lang. The Liberal Democrats were also optimistic of their chances in Kincardine & Deeside and Edinburgh West until recent local Council results rained on their parade. Still, Conservative MPs Buchanan-Smith and Douglas-Hamilton cannot afford to be complacent.

The main issues on which the Scottish seats will be won and lost inevitably include unemployment, housing, transport, education and health. The political fall-out from the poll tax is still landing, and the steel closures at Rosyth and Ravenscraig will not be forgotten quickly. The siting of nuclear weapons and plants, and constitutional reform are also live issues and none of these bode well for the Conservative Party.

One SNP prospective candidate, Roseanna Cunningham says, 'In Scotland it's not so much *Can the Tories Lose?* as *Who's Going to Take their Seats?*'. But then the Scots have rejected the Conservatives before, and still found themselves with four more years of Tory Government. It is open to question whether it is tenable, in even the medium term, for a nation to reject a particular political party so comprehensively and yet still be governed by them.

AYR

Con maj 182:

Con	20,942	39.4%
Lab	20,760	39.1%
Lib	7,859	14.8%
SNP	3,548	6.7%

Swing required 0.2%. **Category** Labour easier win. **MP** George Younger (retiring) **Con PPC** Phil Gallie **Lab PPC** Alistair Osbourne

In George Younger MP, Secretary of State first for Scotland, then Defence, representative of the constituency for over 25 years, the Conservatives had a candidate with that magic combination of high profile, high office and long tenure. Nevertheless, the Tories never felt secure in Ayr, and now that 'Gentleman George' has left politics for the safer business of banking, they should be very worried. Still, two of the things that kept Younger in his seat remain important. First, the population of Ayr which is over 50% middle-class; and second, Ayr's own personal north-south divide.

In the north on the Council estates and around the Commercial harbour Labour hold sway. But Ayr is not called the Bournemouth of the North just for its scenery. The votes in the south around the seaside resorts, the golfing town of Troon and around Prestwick and its airport go to the Tories. The other encouraging thought for Conservatives is that the anti-Thatcher vote in Scotland is no more.

The unenviable task of defending this attractive centre for the 'Burns country' (and birthplace of John Macadam) falls to Phil Gallie, a rightwinger, hydro-power executive and incorrigible optimist. Mr Gallie regularly voices controversial views on local topics: he is credited with bringing the Ulster Tories back into the National Union; he has called for non-payers of poll tax to have their votes taken away; and for Strathclyde Regional staff to be sacked unless they pay up.

Partly for these reasons Labour challenger Alistair Osbourne enjoys public debate with Mr Gallie. Osborne is cut from a different cloth – community worker and former Church of Scotland minister, he demitted in order to fight this seat. With only a 182 margin it is the Conservatives, not Mr Osbourne, who will need God on their side.

DUMFRIES

Con maj 7,493:

Con	18,785	41.9%
Lab	11,292	25.2%
SDP	8,064	18.0%
SNP	6,391	14.2%
Grn	349	0.8%

Swing required 8.4%. **Category** Labour decider. **MP** Sir Hector Monro **Lab PPC** Peter Rennie **Lib Dem PPC** Neil Wallace

Dumfries is an historic town. Mary Queen of Scots spent her last night in Scotland here before her fateful journey south, and Robert Burns is buried in the churchyard of St Michael's.

Farmer, company director and motorbike enthusiast, Sir Hector Monro MP will be one of the more confident Tories north (just) of Hadrians Wall. No great claim you might say, but with a 7,000 majority Dumfries should be the last Conservative seat to fall. That doesn't mean it won't fall but a middle-class population and high owner-occupation, plus the long Tory tradition, suggest that this mainly rural seat will remain Tory.

Dumfries borders on Cumbria and its wide open spaces, and Gretna Green, make for a fair tourist trade. The other principal industries are forestry and agriculture. There is Labour support on the Council estates in Dumfries, but the boundary changes that removed another 10,000 potential supporters in 1983 probably put this one beyond Labour grasp.

EASTWOOD

Con maj 6,014:

Con	19,388	39.5%
SDP	13,374	27.2%
Lab	12,305	25.1%
SNP	4,033	8.2%

Swing required 6.2%. **Category** Liberal Democrat target. **MP** Allan Stewart **Lib Dem PPC** Moira Craig **Lab PPC** Peter Grant-Hutchinson

There are no Conservative seats in Glasgow, but to the south-west of the city the Tories enjoy their safest fortress in the country. Eastwood is a dormitory suburb with the highest proportion of professional and managerial workers of any constituency in Scotland and a long Conservative tradition.

Attempting to breach it will be solicitor Peter Grant-Hutchinson for the Labour Party, working from a power base of Labour support in the industrial town of Barrhead. First across the drawbridge, however, will probably be Liberal Democrat Moira Craig. Still, Allan Stewart, economist and mainstay of the Scottish Office, will likely notch up his fourth consecutive win unless one of the pretenders can significantly squeeze the other's vote.

EDINBURGH PENTLANDS

Con maj 3,745:			
	Con	17,278	38.3%
	Lab	13,533	30.0%
	SDP	11,072	24.5%
	SNP	3,264	7.2%

Swing required 4.2%. **Category** Labour easier win. **MP** Malcolm Rifkind **Lab PPC** Mark Lazarowicz **Lib Dem PPC** Keith Smith **SNP PPC** Kathleen Caskie

The spawling concrete Council estate Wester Hailes is nothing like elegant central Edinburgh and does not appear a likely Conservative seat. The reason for Malcolm Rifkind's tenure in this constituency, which lies to the south of Edinburgh and runs inland to the borders of Lothian, is two-fold.

First, are the deep social divisons in Pentland. The seat also contains suburban and affluent areas overlooked by the Pentland Hills, including the village of Colinton, frequented by Robert Louis Stevenson in his youth.

Second, counting in Rifkind's favour is his reputation, wide respect and eloquence. He has remained relatively untarred by the Thatcherite brush while remaining in the Government.

Labour and the Liberal Democrats vie with each other for second place, leaving the Transport Secretary with a relatively comfortable majority of nearly 4,000 even after a swing to Labour of 4.5% in 1987. Veteran of Edinburgh politics Mark Lazarowicz, however, is well aware that a similar swing this time will remove the most articulate spokesperson of Scottish Conservatism, particularly if the Scots tradition of tactical voting continues.

EDINBURGH WEST

Con maj 1,234:	Con 18,450	37.4%
	Lib 17,216	34.9%
	Lab 10,957	22.2%
	SNP 2,774	5.6%

Swing required 1.8%. **Category** Liberal Democrat target. **MP** Lord James Douglas-Hamilton **Lib Dem PPC** Donald Gorrie **Lab PPC** Irene Kitson **SNP PPC** Graham Sutherland

Edinburgh West Tory MP Lord James Douglas-Hamilton is popularly known as 'Lucky Jim' following close shaves in the last two general elections. Wielding the razor then were the Liberals, and they have again set their hearts and their sights on this seat bordering on the Firth of Forth. Their champion is Donald Gorrie: probably the best-known Liberal Democrat in Edinburgh, he is a veteran of regional and district Councils. Standing on a ticket that calls for PR and a Scottish Parliament plus a defence of local democracy, his success will depend on whether he can win a tactical squeeze on the Labour vote.

Vice versa Irene Kitson for Labour will need a squeeze on the Liberal vote. She is trying to get it by insisting that Labour are the real challengers to Mr Douglas-Hamilton as proven by their success in the 1989 regional elections. As well as attacking the Tories on poll tax, the health service and the economy the Labour campaign makes education a priority issue. This is appropriate as Edinburgh West is the home of Miss Jean Brodie and prides itself on its excellent schools. With Graham Sutherland also in the running for the SNP the vote against the Conservatives is thoroughly split.

The current make up of Edinburgh West, however, bodes well for Douglas-Hamilton. Boundary changes have pushed the decrepit estates over the line into Leith while those remaining are the most up-market in the Capital. The seat is now a thoroughly middle-class residential district, home to Edinburgh's upper orders and this suits Lord James Douglas-Hamilton just fine. Still it will be a hard-fought battle and 'Gentleman Jim' will need his Oxford boxing blue just as much as his Eton and Balliol background.

GALLOWAY & UPPER NITHSDALE

Con maj 3,673:	Con 16,592	40.3%
	SNP 12,919	31.5%
	Lib 6,001	14.6%
	Lab 5,298	12.9%

Swing required 4.4%. **Category** Scottish National target. **MP** Ian Lang **SNP PPC** Matt Brown **Lib Dem PPC** John McKerchar **Lab PPC** Gordon Dangerfield

the latter being 30 year-old Liberal Democrat Nicol Stephen. But with Labour, SNP and the Green Party also running, it is a five-cornered contest. This combination of a split opposition, a new improved Prime Minister and his own reputation, leaves Buchanan-Smith hopeful.

PERTH & KINROSS

Con maj 5,676:

Con	18,716	39.6%
SNP	13,040	27.6%
Lib	7,969	16.9%
Lab	7,490	15.9%

Swing required 6%. **Category** Scottish National target. **MP** Nicholas Fairbairn **SNP PPC** Roseanna Cunningham **Lib Dem PPC** Malcolm Black **Lab PPC** Merv Rolse

Nicholas Fairbairn is a MP known to his friends as colourful and to his opponents as eccentric and extreme. Whichever you choose, it will take more than namecalling to unseat him. The Nationalists have targetted this constituency and fielded one of their best candidates, Roseanna Cunningham. Ms Cunningham, an advocate by profession, has noted a potential in the constituency for tactical voting against a 'kenspeckle character'.

Still, the facts are that Perth & Kinross is in a prosperous part of lowland Scotland with low unemployment – Conservative country. Combining the city of Perth and old Kinross, the economy is vibrant with most people earning a living in either whisky, oil, agriculture or tourism. Malcolm Black will fight the Liberal Democrat corner, and Merve Rolse the Labour, but this should be a Tory/Nationalist bout.

STIRLING

Con maj 548:

Con	17,191	38.3%
Lab	16,643	36.2%
Lib	6,804	14.8%
SNP	4,897	10.7%

Swing required 1.1%. **Category** Labour easier win. **MP** Michael Forsyth **Lab PPC** Kate Phillips

The battle of Bannockburn was fought in Stirling and if Labour has its way the election this year will be no less dramatic. Labour has placed rightwing Scottish Office minister Michael Forsyth at the head of its hit list. The Stirling MP is the man that Labour love to hate and his slim 548 majority brings him well within their grasp this time around.

The Labour candidate charged with teaching him a lesson is educational consultant Kate Phillips. She claims that his hard-line views have alienated even his own supporters, and that his opinions on the NHS and education in particular will help lose him the election.

In his favour Forsyth has the new-look Government in Westminster and his own much-respected campaigns office, staffed by professionals ready, they claim, for an election at any time. Their knowledge of this large and sprawling constituency and their own strengths and weaknesses will make a difference, but whether it will be enough to pull Michael Forsyth through is another matter.

TAYSIDE NORTH

Con maj 5,016:

Con	18,307	45.4%
SNP	13,291	32.9%
Lib	5,201	12.9%
Lab	3,550	8.8%

Swing required 6.3%. **Category** Scottish National target. **MP** William Walker **SNP PPC** John Swinney **Lib Dem PPC** Simon Horner **Lab PPC** Stewart Maclennan

While many Scottish Tories are celebrating the end of the Thatcher years, Tayside North MP Bill Walker is looking a little out-of-place in this new era of moderation and diplomacy. Although Walker is King of the colourful and idiosyncratic opinion, and beloved of newspaper editors looking for headlines and quotable quotes, there is no doubt that he has alienated a significant number of supporters down the years.

So in what should be Tory heartland the SNP are in with a chance and they are taking it seriously. Their local party machine is tried and tested, with their chosen candidate SNP national secretary John Swinney. Among the issues they are focusing on are transport, nuclear dumping and especially the controversial A9 road. Their secret weapon, though, is Walker himself whom the SNP believe could talk himself out of a job. Meanwhile, the Labour and Liberal Democrat candidates will battle for third place with candidates Stewart McLennan and Simon Horner respectively.

SOUTH

In the 1987 general election, there was a swing to the Conservatives in the south of England although the national swing saw Labour making up ground from the debacle of 1983. After the 1987 general election, excluding London, there were only three Labour seats left south of the line between the Wash and the Severn estuary (Oxford East, Norwich South and Bristol South).

The reasons for this are very straightforward. The south of England is the part of the United Kingdom which benefited most from the economic growth of the Thatcher years. Traditional Labour loyalties were undermined in working-class seats, as far apart as Swindon and Harlow, by a sense of economic improvement, the encouragement of home ownership through Council-house sales, and the emergence of the SDP. Voters became more pragmatic, not necessarily lost to Labour, but wanting to shop around.

More well-to-do seats saw the Alliance slip past Labour into the role of challenging the Tories and a tendency for the Labour vote to be squeezed. But this has yet to produce MPs for the Liberal Democrats, other than Eastbourne which was captured in the peculiar circumstances of a by-election. Oxford in 1987 saw the clearest example in England of tactical voting in a general election, and it remains the case that many Conservative MPs, especially in the marginal seats, have been elected on minority votes: only in Cambridge and Stevenage is it in any way unclear which Party is the challenger.

The success of the Conservatives in the South was very much perceived as the basis for the Thatcherite ascendancy of the 1980s. It is still the case that if the Conservatives hold the South, including London, they are unlikely to lose the election.

The opposition argues that Conservative ascendancy has not been produced by any radical transformation of social attitudes. Certainly, voting in Council elections – both for the Liberal Democrats and for Labour – shows that there is still support in the South for public services where delivered efficiently and imaginatively.

The key to the outcome of the election in the south lies in the economy. Do voters in the key marginals still believe that 'there is no alternative'? Or, with record mortgage interest rates and the return of recession, will sufficient numbers of voters desert the Conservatives because they no longer believe they are the most effective economic managers?

BASILDON

Con maj 2,649:

Con 21,858 43.5%
Lab 19,209 38.3%
Lib 9,139 18.2%

Swing required 2.6%. **Category** Labour easier win. **MP** David Amess **Lab PPC** John Potter **Lib Dem PPC** Geoff Williams

The disappointment on the face of Labour candidate Julian Fulbrook, relayed to millions on television, was an early indication on election night 11 June 1987 that Labour had failed to win Basildon, an 'easier win' seat even then, and that they were therefore set for an uncomfortable night.

Basildon is the classic Essex boom town, its skilled workers wooed by the Conservatives through the promise of economic prosperity and a 'property-owning democracy'. Executive recruitment manager David Amess is a highly articulate, almost suave, rightish Conservative with his finger on the popular pulse.

Although still technically an 'easier win' for Labour, Basildon is a key test as to whether Labour can demonstrate its credentials in economic management. Its dominance on the local Council will not necessarily translate into votes when the government of the country is at stake.

CAMBRIDGE

Con maj 5,060:

Con 21,624 40.0%
SDP 16,564 30.6%
Lab 15,319 28.3%

Swing required 4.7% to Lib Dems; 5.9% to Lab. **Category** three way marginal. **MP** Robert Rhodes James (retiring) **Con PPC** Mark Bishop **Lib Dem PPC** David Howarth **Lab PPC** Anne Campbell

The Alliance result in 1987 was probably boosted by the candidature of Shirley Williams, though some have suggested that her record as Labour Education Secretary may have lost some votes in this ancient, very privileged university city in the fens.

Both Labour and the Liberal Democrats have chosen PPCs with a County Council flavour. Anne Campbell is a former County Councillor and David Howarth a current one. Should the Liberal Democrat revival continue, there is a real danger that Ms Campbell and Mr Howarth will shoot one another out of the water.

Robert Rhodes James, Churchill biographer and MP of 15 years, is retiring, though he is still only in his 50s. His would-be successor, Mark Bishop, is a lawyer who was formerly active in the Cambridge students' union. A lively contest, more informed than most, can be expected in what still appears a genuine three way marginal.

CAMBRIDGESHIRE NORTH EAST

Con maj 1,428:

Con	26,983	47.0%
Lib	25,555	44.5%
Lab	4,891	8.5%

Swing required 1.8%. **Category** Liberal Democrat target. **MP** Malcolm Moss **Lib Dem PPC** Maurice Leeke **Lab PPC** Ronald Harris

As with most Liberal seats, there was a significant personal vote in the Fens for 'Just a Minute' contributor and gourmet Clement Freud who won a by-election in 1973 and held on until the last general election. Local man Malcolm Moss, his successor, quickly won a high reputation in the House of Commons.

There can be no doubt, however, that the Liberal Democrats remain the challenger in the seat. Their PPC, County Councillor Maurice Leeke, has generated considerable local publicity recently, and his local Party has seen a marked increase in membership. Mr Leeke will need a fair head of steam if he is to oust the Fenlands imcumbent.

CHELMSFORD

Con maj 7,761:

Con	35,231	51.9%
Lib	27,470	40.5%
Lab	4,642	6.8%
Grn	486	0.7%

Swing required 5.7%. **Category** Liberal Democrat target. **MP** Simon Burns **Lib Dem PPC** Hugh Nicholson **Lab PPC** Roy Chad

Chelmsford is the fast-growing county town of the equally fast-growing county of Essex. At the 1983 boundary review, a rather odd shaped constituency emerged, but when Norman St John Stevas stepped down in 1987, the growth of new houses provided fertile ground for the youngish Tory Simon Burns. Whereas his predecessor had hung on in 1983 by only 378 votes, Mr Burns won a healthy majority of nearly 8,000.

Chelmsford is one of a number of seats which has always appeared on the Liberals' target list but has never quite delivered. And although the Liberals have been strong in local elections, they have retreated more recently, losing four of their five county seats in 1989.

Given the circumstances, the Liberal Democrat Hugh Nicholson, standing for the first time, will probably find it tough to hold the 40% from 1987.

CHELTENHAM

Con majority 4,896:

Con	31,371	50.2%
Lib	26,475	42.3%
Lab	4,701	7.5%

Swing required 3.9%. **Category** Liberal Democrat target. **MP** Sir Charles Irving (retiring) **Con PPC** John Taylor **Lib Dem PPC** Nigel Jones **Lab PPC** Pam Tatlow

Reaction from some local Tories to the selection of black Birmingham barrister John Taylor catapulted this Cotswolds spa town into the national press and TV. It is difficult to judge how much of that reaction was due to Mr Taylor's colour, how much to the fact that Cheltenham has always had a local MP, and how much to the fact that the local Tory Party leadership offered the members a shortlist with only one name.

The Liberal Democrats are well placed to take advantage of any dissident Tory vote. Their prospective candidate Nigel Jones was born in Cheltenham and in a quiet, unassuming manner he is burrowing away in the traditional community-based Liberal way. The local Party follows the advice of the late David Penhaligon -'If you have something to say write it on a piece of paper and put it through letter-boxes'. In the May 1990 local elections, the Liberal Democrats won 8 out of 11 seats.

Labour's vote has declined consistently since 1979. Their PPC Pam Tatlow, a Bristol City Councillor, intends to revive it by stressing that only Labour can form an alternative Government.

The Tory leadership, John Major and Chris Patten included, have strongly supported Mr Taylor who is unquestionably an able and intelligent politician, but doubts linger as to whether this is the best seat for him. If the Liberal Democrats can continue their post-Ribble poll improvement, this looks like one of their best opportunities to capture a Conservative seat.

CORBY

Con maj 1,805:

Con	23,323	44.3%
Lab	21,518	40.9%
Lib	7,803	14.8%

Swing required 1.7%. **Category** Labour easier win. **MP** William Powell **Lab PPC** Sandy Feather **Lib Dem PPC** Melvyn Roffe

The constituency divides roughly half-and-half between Corby town and a rural swathe of Northamptonshire including Oundle public school (where Liberal Democrat Melvyn Roffe is a teacher). The town made national headlines in the early 1980s with the closure of its steelworks, but its proximity to London, the Midlands and the east coast ports have led to its development as a distribution centre for electronic components, Pilkington Glass and Oxford University Press. Corby town has remained a Labour stronghold.

The Labour PPC, Sandy Feather, lives in the village of Sudborough. His desire to protect hedgerows and concern over speculative building development reveal a commitment to rural life not always at the forefront of Labour politics but particularly relevant to this kind of seat.

Concern over the future of Kettering Hospital, the opting out of Kingswood School in Corby, the launch of a Community Technology College, and a housing shortage, give a wide range of contentious local issues. But the return of unemployment in 1991 suggests that the economy may turn out to be the decisive factor here. William Powell will be hoping that the Government can 'get it right'.

DOVER
Con maj 6,541:

Con	25,343	46.0%
Lab	18,802	34.1%
SDP	10,942	19.9%

Swing required 6.0%. **Category** Labour decider. **MP** David Shaw **Lab PPC** Gywn Prosser

Chartered accountant David Shaw's majority in this seat is very vulnerable to the Government's neglect of its local economy. In 1989 British Coal closed the last pit in the Kent coalfield, Bettshanger, despite its excellent reserves of coal. Though the construction of the Channel Tunnel has brought a kind of superficial prosperity to the constituency, the underlying unemployment and future uncertainty for cross-channel shipping combine to make Dover a serious Labour target.

However, the local Labour organisation will have to increase its commitment and professionalism to win back the large number of supporters who defected to the SDP in the early 1980s. The 1987 result saw Labour's vote up by 3.3%, but the SDP 19.9% remains a formidable chunk of the electorate. Mr Shaw succeeded to the seat in 1987, and has not been particularly prominent as a new boy. Dover is Labour's best prospect in Kent, and a win here would show that Labour has moved out of its Northern laager.

EASTBOURNE

Con maj 16,923:		
	Con 33,587	59.9%
	Lib 16,664	29.7%
	Lab 4,928	8.8%
	Grn 867	1.5%

Swing required 15.1%. **Category** Liberal Democrat target. **MP** David Bellotti (Lib Dem) **Con PPC** Nigel Waterson

This quiet south coast resort was traditionally a safe Conservative seat. It was held from 1974 by Ian Gow until he was assassinated by the Provisional IRA in 1990. The subsequent by-election produced a sensational Liberal Democrat victory.

Mr Bellotti's local party has been signing up many new members. Unlike Ribble Valley (where the Liberals won a by-election in March 1991), the Eastbourne victory came on the back of a sustained record by the Liberals in local government. Mr Bellotti was known as a County Councillor.

However, the Conservatives are unlikely to run as inept a campaign as they did in the by-election, especially as they have replaced Richard Hickmet with a new PPC. With voters' minds distracted by the television battle between Mr Major and Mr Kinnock, Mr Bellotti will have his work cut out to hold the seat.

GRAVESHAM

Con maj 8,792:		
	Con 28,891	50.1%
	Lab 20,099	34.8%
	Lib 8,724	15.1%

Swing required 7.7%. **Category** Labour decider. **MP** Jacques Arnold **Lab PPC** Graham Green

The 1983 Boundary Commission changes meant that former Gravesend became Gravesham, and that an apparently easy Conservative win became more problematic. The lost territory was Tory heartland, and the Conservative MP Timothy Brinton actually saw his majority reduced in the 1983 general election.

Whilst the new Conservative candidate, international banker Jacques Arnold, actually increased his vote in 1987, the seat remains a Labour target. But the pockets of Labour strength (particularly in Gravesend) are not enough on their own, and PPC Graham Green will need to woo floating voters in more inland, rural places like Shorne and Higham.

The seat changed hands three times between 1964 and 1979, following the changes in government. Labour must win seats like Gravesham if they are to form an overall majority.

HARLOW

Con maj 5,877:

Con	26,017	47.2%
Lab	20,140	36.6%
SDP	8,915	16.2%

Swing required 5.3%. **Category** Labour decider. **MP** Jerry Hayes **Lab PPC** Bill Rammell **Lib Dem PPC** Lorna Spenceley

The vintage Labour MP, Stan Newens, lost this seat in 1983 and failed to regain it in 1987. It may have been that his status as a Member of the European Parliament put the electorate off, or it may have been his distinctive time-warp character – he has the air of an avuncular, tweeded schoolmaster lecturing his potential supporters about the moral rectitude of socialism.

This time around, the PPC is an energetic, youthful local councillor, Bill Rammell, who is already giving Conservative incumbent Jerry Hayes a run for his money by leading non-partisan all-in campaigns over local schools, housing and NHS cuts. Whilst the sale of Council houses was a contentious issue in 1983, Mr Rammell thinks that Labour has subsequently regained its solid support in the new town, which comprises 6/7ths of the constituency. He intends to work hard, however, to challenge the Liberal Democrats in the rural villages which make up the remaining seventh.

Although Jeremy Hayes, who achieved an increased majority in 1987, has cultivated a reputation as a 'wet', and is an effective television performer, his voting record has generally been foursquare behind the government. Mr Rammell remembers with relish his one public debate with Mr Hayes, when local council housing tenants rounded on the MP, and Hayes has thus far avoided further public encounters.

As with other 'new town' southern seats, much here will depend on voters' perception of their own material interest and thus on their judgement of the prospects for the economy under Labour or the Conservatives.

IPSWICH

Con maj 874:

Con	23,328	44.4%
Lab	22,454	42.7%
SDP	6,596	12.6%
Oth	174	0.3%

Swing required 0.9%. **Category** Labour easier win. **MP** Michael Irvine **Lab PPC** Jamie Cann

Suffolk's county town was known for many years as 'Ips-weetch' because of the popularity and respect afforded to its intelligent and pragmatic MP, Ken Weetch.

The defeat of Mr Weetch, therefore, by Rugby-educated solicitor Michael Irvine was something of a surprise.

With improved rail links with London, there have been gradual demographic changes, both with insurance companies bringing white-collar employment to the town and with growing numbers commuting to London. Ipswich affectionately thinks of itself as being 'a little bit behind' more cosmopolitan places, and this in itself might account for the shift to the right occurring in 1987 rather than earlier. In addition, the very success of the national campaign for Labour that year may have concentrated the minds of voters on the 'dangers' of a Labour Government rather than on the virtues of Mr Weetch as a constituency MP.

Labour's new PPC Jamie Cann is well-known locally as a former Council leader and deputy head of a primary school. Mr Cann has now left the Council to concentrate on the campaign against Mr Irvine. A close-fought contest seems likely.

ISLE OF WIGHT

Con maj 6,442:

Con	40,175	51.2%
Lib	33,733	43.0%
Lab	4,626	5.9%

Swing required 4.1%. **Category** Liberal Democrat target. **MP** Barry Field **Lib Dem PPC** Peter Brand **Lab PPC** Kenn Pearson

The Isle of Wight was held for the Liberals by Stephen Ross from 1974. He stood down in 1987 and went to the House of Lords. With the removal of Mr Ross's personal vote, built up through hard work on behalf of his constituents, some concluded that Mr Field, the House of Commons' only undertaker, had laid to rest Liberal Democrat hopes of regaining the seat. The Liberal PPC, however, Peter Brand, is well-known as Deputy Leader of the administration running the County Council. The island is also currently acting as a guinea pig for the metering of tap water, which many feel adds insult to the injury of the poll tax.

The Liberal Democrats can be expected to put up a strong challenge and may be able to squeeze the Labour vote back to its all-time 1983 low of 2.4%.

LUTON SOUTH

Con maj 5,115:

Con	24,762	46.2%
Lab	19,647	36.7%
Lib	9,146	17.1%

Swing required 4.9%. **Category** Labour decider. **MP** Graham Bright **Lab PPC** Bill McKenzie

Graham Bright, who has represented the seat since 1979, is now John Major's parliamentary private secretary. He is less well-known than Luton's other MP John Carlisle who championed the cause of sporting links with South Africa through the years of apartheid boycott. But Mr Bright has a strong professional interest in weight loss – as Chairman of Dietary Foods Ltd – and in parliamentary consideration of aviation issues, which is not surprising given that Luton South contains the airport immortalised by Lorraine Chase.

Labour's Bill McKenzie, a former partner at Price Waterhouse, has been a Luton District Councillor for 16 years. He is an advisor to Labour's John Smith and Gordon Brown, and would bring an expertise on taxation to Westminster. Labour has real strongholds in this mainly working-class constituency which has a 20% ethnic minority population, including a Kashmiri Muslim community.

This is a seat where Mr McKenzie's sort of candidate should be able to squeeze the centre vote if Labour is coming over well nationally and if the Government is failing to deliver on the economic issues. A Conservative defeat in Luton South would be likely to indicate the end of Mr Major's majority in the Commons. A seat to watch.

MILTON KEYNES SOUTH WEST

Con maj 13,701:	Con 35,396 47.8%
(old 'Milton Keynes'	SDP 21,695 29.3%
seat)	Lab 16,111 21.1%

Swing required [–] **Category** Labour decider. **MP** William Benyon (retiring) **Con PPC** Barry Legg **Lab PPC** Kevin Wilson **Lib Dem** Martin Burke

Because of the increasing numbers of escapees from the London fug, the newest new town had become seriously under-represented with just one MP. In January 1989, the Boundary Commission recommended that Milton Keynes be carved into two seats. Of the two, Milton Keynes South West looks the more vulnerable for the Tories. Local election results in 1988 (at district level) and 1989 (at county level) showed Labour well ahead in the wards allocated to this new constituency. Wolverton, a surviving relic of the railway's greatness, actually returned the only Labour county councillor in Buckinghamshire.

Nevertheless, Labour will have to do exceptionally well to deprive the Tory PPC, Barry Legg, of his inheritance from William Benyon. Labour is much better placed than the Liberal Democrats in this seat but will be unable to erode the Tory lead without substantial tactical voting, or a dramatic upsurge in Labour loyalism from the leafy glades of the new town.

NORTH EAST MILTON KEYNES

Con maj: see Milton Keynes South West
Swing required [–] **Category** Liberal Democrat target. **Con PPC**
Peter Butler **Lib Dem PPC** Peter Gaskell **Lab PPC** Maggie Cosin

The second new Milton Keynes seat is the more 'rural', hence the Boundary Commission's decision to put 'North East' before 'Milton Keynes'. In local elections the former Alliance parties did better than either the major parties in the wards contested.

Nevertheless, Conservative PPC Peter Butler must be firm favourite to succeed as robust Camden Councillor Maggie Cosin (who campaigned forcefully against Chingford's Norman Tebbit in 1987) is unlikely to be squeezed. The constituency includes the old borough of Newport Pagnell, the village wards of Lavendon and Olney, the green belt Woburn Sands and the growing Milton Keynes wards of Linfrod, Bradwell and Pineham. There would seem to be enough Conservative votes for Mr Butler to be comfortably ahead in a three way fight.

NORTHAMPTON NORTH

Con maj 9,816:		
	Con 24,816	48.0%
	Lab 15,560	30.1%
	Lib 10,690	20.7%
	Grn 471	0.9%
	Oth 156	0.3%

Swing required 9%. **Category** Labour decider. **MP** Tony Marlow
Lab PPC Janet Thomas **Lib Dem PPC** Richard Church

Northampton North is the last seat, other than the special cases of Milton Keynes South West and Mid Staffs, which makes the 'decider seat' category. Should Labour win here, there would very probably be a majority Labour Government.

That said, since Tony Marlow first took the seat from left-winger Maureen Colquhoun in 1979, his majority has increased to nearly five figures. Mr Marlow is a defence expert with a competent air and high media profile. Unfortunately for him, however, this profile has not always been favourable as one tabloid has made hay with his complicated private life; his identification with the Palestinian cause was not flavour of the month during the Gulf crisis; and his remarks in the House about 'headaches' during the discussions of the 'rape in marriage' Bill may not have gone down too well with local women voters.

Given the last point, Labour's choice of Janet Thomas may turn out to have been a shrewd one. Mrs Thomas has represented since 1981 the part of the constituency in which she lives. She has also sat on the Regional Health Authority and Anglian Water, indicating a community-type rather than a career-type politican motivated to stand for Parliament for the first time in her early 50s by 'the damage done by 12 years of Tory Government' and her 'determination to get them out'.

Northampton North is a 'working class with middle class aspirations' kind of new town with recently built private housing estates. Its voters plumped in 1983 and 1987 for the rosy vision of economic growth and the 'property-owning democracy', but mortgage rates and recession are undermining the Tory dream.

Given the nature of the seat, its importance as an indicator of the overall general election result and the contrast in style of the two major contenders, this has the makings of a classic encounter. Given Mr Marlow's politics, it is perhaps surprising he did not support Mrs Thatcher in the leadership contest – but given his sense for political survival, perhaps it is not.

NORWICH NORTH

Con maj 7,776:

Con 22,772 45.8%
Lab 14,996 30.2%
Lib 11,922 24.0%

Swing required 7.8%. **Category** Labour decider. **MP** Patrick Thompson **Lab PPC** Ian Gibson **Lib Dem PPC** David Harrison

Apart from Oxford East, Norwich South was Labour's only 1987 gain south of the line from the Wash to the Severn estuary. In the North seat, there was a swing of 1.7% the other way. This can be accounted for partly by a pronounced effect of 'double incumbency' (the previous Labour MP and former minister, David Ennals, had a large personal vote). For both 1983 and 1987 boundary changes had weakened Labour's position, and indeed Mr Ennals would not have held on in 1979 had the new boundaries come along earlier.

Another fly in the ointment for Labour is the strength of the centre, who surged up in 1983 at Labour's expense and more than held their ground four years later. The initial battle in this socially diverse constituency will be between Ian Gibson and David Harrison. Former teacher and engineer Patrick Thompson is the likely beneficiary.

OXFORD WEST & ABINGDON

Con maj 4,878:   Con 25,171   46.4%

SDP 20,293   37.4%

Lab 8,108   14.9%

Swing required 4.5%. **Category** Liberal Democrat target. **MP** John Patten **Lib Dem PPC** Sir William Goodhart **Lab PPC** Bruce Kent

Sir William Goodhart is contesting this seat for the first time. His predecessor, Christopher Huhne, gave John Patten a good run for his money. The constituency takes in the local groves of the academy, and Oxford students were much taken by the desire to vote tactically against the Conservatives. Indeed tactical voting became a city-wide issue, with a marked impact in both of the constituencies. In the more industrial Oxford East, the Conservative Steven Norris lost his seat to Labour against the regional trend, and in Oxford West Huhne increased the SDP vote by 4%.

The Liberal Democrats are taking this constituency very seriously indeed. They have a full-time agent in place, and much attention is being paid to the Abingdon wards, where a high number of technical-professional voters are apparently disgruntled by the Government's neglect of scientific research. Though John Patten is a Government minister, his real hold over the seat is his long-term local connection. Sir William Goodhart has returned to his childhood roots to fight Oxford West and certainly believes he can win.

The Labour PPC Bruce Kent will doubtless fight the seat with characteristic vigour and commitment. He may woo some of the student vote back from Goodhart. However, the local Party organisation has yet to show itself as keen to fight as its candidate. In seats like this, local Labour inertia may be determined by a sneaking, secret desire to see the Tory turfed out! Such *de facto* pragmatism remains the hard, unspoken reality of unseating the Tories in a three party system.

PETERBOROUGH

Con maj 9,784:   Con 30,624   49.4%

Lab 20,840   33.6%

Lib 9,984   16.1%

Grn 506   0.8%

Swing required 7.9%. **Category** Labour decider. **MP** Brian Mawhinney **Lab PPC** Julie Owens

It is a sobering fact for fans of majority Labour Governments that Mr Kinnock could win Peterborough and still be short of the magic figure of 326. It was held for Labour from 1974 to 1979, but its 'new town' population moved, like so many others in the south, to the Conservatives in the 1980s.

Church of England Synod member, Brian Mawhinney is a moderate MP with interests in the 'caring' issues. Julie Owens, who works for the Socialist Group in the European Parliament, will need the impetus of a very strong national trend to remove him.

PORTSMOUTH SOUTH

Con maj 205:

Con 23,534	43.3%
SDP 23,329	42.9%
Lab 7,047	13.0%
Oth 455	0.8%

Swing required 0.2%. **Category** Liberal Democrat target. **MP** David Martin **Lib Dem PPC** Mike Hancock **Lab PPC** Sally Thomas

Mike Hancock contested the seat for the SDP in 1983, came 12,000 behind Conservative Bonner Pink, won the seat in a by-election in 1984 and then lost by 205 votes in the 1987 election, despite managing to squeeze the Labour vote.

He has been selected as PPC by the Liberal Democrats to tussle once again with David Martin, but the omens are not good. Portsmouth South was traditionally a safe Tory seat, and is certainly not as vulnerable to the Liberal Democrats as the 1987 majority might suggest. That said, Mike Hancock is a capable campaigner and still well-known in the area as an active local Councillor.

SLOUGH

Con maj 4,090:

Con 26,166	46.9%
Lab 22,076	39.6%
SDP 7,490	13.4%

Swing required 3.7%. **Category** Labour easier win. **MP** John Watts **Lab PPC** Eddie Lopez

Slough is famous for Mars Bars and a John Betjeman poem that was less than enthusiastic about its architecture. Its elongated shape reveals the importance of both the London-to-Bath road and the Great Western Railway in the town's origins.

Slough mushroomed around an army equipment dump after the Great War, and in the 1930s new industries attracted migrants from the depressed regions of the North and South Wales. More recently, it has attracted a large Asian population.

As a fairly prosperous industrial town, Slough illustrates Labour's problems in the south. In the 1950s and 60s its MP was Fenner Brockway, champion of colonial independence, and he was followed from 1966 to 1983 by Joan Lestor, now Labour MP for Eccles in Lancashire.

By the 1980s Labour loyalties were being weakened by the sale of Council homes and the establishment of the SDP. A rightward swing led to the victory of Conservative John Watts in 1983, and he went on to an increased majority of over 4,000 in 1987.

Slough still elects an overwhelmingly Labour Council, which suggests that an important section of voters follow whichever party they feel best serves their interests in any particular election. Mr Kinnock will need to convince them of his Party's ability to manage the economy if Labour is to regain this seat.

SOUTHAMPTON ITCHEN

Con maj 6,716:

Con	24,419	44.3%
Lab	17,703	32.1%
SDP	13,006	23.6%

Swing required 6.1%. **Category** Labour decider. **MP** Christopher Chope **Lab PPC** John Denham **Lib Dem PPC** James Hodgson

Southampton Itchen, like Southampton Test, was an almost exact replica of the overall national vote in 1987. This may, however, be a transitory phenomenon, as Labour were recovering from the defection to the SDP in 1981 of the sitting MP Richard Mitchell. Mr Mitchell managed second place in 1983 but slipped back to third in 1987.

Labour's PPC John Denham will therefore feel entitled to the 'effective challenger to the Tories' berth and confident of an above-average swing, provided that he can continue the squeeze on Councillor James Hodgson. Christopher Chope was the privatisation-trailblazing Leader of Wandsworth Council before he entered Parliament – his tenure in Itchen is less secure than it looks.

SOUTHAMPTON TEST

Con maj 6,954:

Con	25,722	45.6%
Lab	18,768	33.3%
Lib	11,950	21.2%

Swing required 6.2%. **Category** Labour decider. **MP** James Hill **Lab PPC** Alan Whithead

Southampton Test is to the west of Itchen and is marginally more middle-class. James Hill held the seat from 1970 to October 1974, lost it (to Bryan Gould), got it back in 1979 and hasn't let go. He has served two spells as a City Councillor when he hasn't been in Parliament, so is well-known to locals.

Also something of a local landmark is Alan Whitehead the Leader of the Labour-controlled Council since 1984. With the March announcement of the £140 off poll tax bills, Mr Whitehead was able to say the reduction would be £155 in Southampton because non-payment was lower than expected and because the Council had followed a 'financially prudent course' – this 'John Smith of Southampton' performance seems well suited to the seat.

STEVENAGE

Con maj 5,340:

Con	23,541 42.1%
SDP	18,201 32.5%
Lab	14,229 25.4%

Swing required 4.8% for Lib Dem, 8.4% for Lab. **Category** three way marginal. **MP** Timothy Wood **Lib Dem PPC** Andrew Reilly **Lab PPC** Judith Church

The constituency encompasses one of the postwar new towns on the northern fringes of London. In the days of rampant Thatcherism it was asserted that such new towns, with their preponderance of skilled workers, were becoming permanently blue, and that the Labour hold, successfully exported from the East End, Islington and Camden, had been uprooted.

In Stevenage, Labour's Judith Church resolutely disputes this claim. She views the coming contest as a straight fight against the incumbent Tory, Tim Wood, even though the SDP came second in 1987. Stevenage was 'never' Liberal territory, and the serious haemorrhage for Labour occurred when their MP, Shirley Williams, defected to the SDP. Ben Stoneham, the local candidate who fought for the SDP in 1983 and 1987, is not standing again, and Andrew Reilly is the second PPC the Liberal Democrats have had to choose. Previous SDP representation on the council has not translated well into the Liberal Democrats, who have not been fielding candidates in many wards.

Judith Church is a squeaky clean Labour PPC, likeable and keen to win. She believes that indifference towards the redundancies in British Aerospace and ICL has combined with high interest rates to make the seat vulnerable to Labour. Timothy Wood was recently quoted in a local paper saying he expected a tough fight this time. Nevertheless, an opinion poll in this constituency would certainly help local voters to determine what their options really are.

SWINDON

Con maj 4,857:
Con 29,385 43.8%
Lab 24,528 36.6%
SDP 13,114 19.6%

Swing required 3.6%. **Category** Labour easier win. **MP** Simon Coombs **Lab PPC** Jim D'Avila

Swindon grew up as a railway town around the workshops of the Great Western Railway built in 1865 by Isambard Kingdom Brunel. Light engineering became a tradition in the town and Rover are still the largest employer.

Its accessibility from London, either by rail or the M4, accounts for the current trend towards service-based industries: firms as varied as WH Smiths, Honda, Allied Dunbar and the Bible Society now situate their headquarters in the town. Proximity to London also explains why Swindon is beloved by the media as 'the marginal to watch'.

As a southern 'boom town', Swindon provides a classic example of skilled workers switching to the Tories in 1983, when Simon Coombs was first elected. Coombs achieved a further swing of 2.4% in 1987, but job losses in 1991 suggest that this is a seat where 'the economy' will be the crucial issue.

Labour meanwhile have remained dominant in local government. Their PPC, Council Deputy Leader, Jim D'Avila rolls his 'r's' in the way you might expect of someone born and bred locally: 'Many people know me, especially with such a funny sounding name, people remember that ...'.

A letter writer to a local paper recently complained that having been delighted to find Mr D'Avila unusually absent from its reportage, went home only to be confronted by his face on regional television news. D'Avila, a Union convenor at Rover, is strongly committed to a positive relationship with the private sector. If Labour cannot win Swindon with such a popular local figure, it is difficult to see how they can win at all.

THURROCK

Con maj 690:
Con 20,527 42.5%
Lab 19,837 41.0%
SDP 7,970 16.6%

Swing required 0.8%. **Category** Labour easier win. **MP** Tim Janman **Lab PPC** Andrew MacKinlay **Lib Dem PPC** Alan Banton

In 1974 Labour had a 10,000 majority in Thurrock. In 1979 it fell to 7,300. By 1983 it was under 2,000, and in 1987 the Tory right-winger Tim Janman snatched the seat.

It is as dramatic an example of Labour collapse as one might find. So why did it happen?

First, the formation of the SDP undermined traditional Labour loyalties. The Tory share of the vote remained fairly static between 1979 and 1983, but Labour lost around 12% to the Social Democrats. After that, the rest was 'easy', and Janman needed a swing of only 2.6% to win in 1987.

Second, Thurrock has a complicated social make-up. It manages to combine a working-class sense of decline, produced by the containerisation of the docks, with the 'working class aspiring middle class' feel of the new towns: both halves of the combination have undermined Labour, particularly when combined with the very *white* nature of the seat and its relative geographical proximity to the Asian areas in the East End. Janman's fierce anti-leftism and his very public opposition to immigration from Hong Kong find echoes among his constituents.

Thurrock is also distinguished both by a very low turn-out in local elections and a new 'Lakeside' shopping centre opened just before Christmas 1990 with parking for 10,000 cars. The container port at Tilbury is easily the largest in London following the closure of the Royal and Surrey Docks. Thurrock seems to exemplify both Labour's 'London problem' and its 'Essex problem'. With the 'double incumbency' effect in his favour for the next election and his proven populist skills, Mr Janman will not be removed anything like as easily as the bare 1987 figures might suggest.

SOUTH WEST

The South West has the full range of political battles, making it one of the most interesting regions for the election.

Bristol is a political litmus paper. When Labour last won a general election, in October 1974, they won four of the five parliamentary seats in the city. Following the decline of traditional industries and a period of party in-fighting, Labour now has only one seat left. In 1987, the Conservatives, against the national trend, gained ground, but with only 44% of the city's vote (and 80% of the city's seats!) they are vulnerable to Labour in East, North West and Kingswood. The Kinnockites have gained the ascendency within the Bristol Labour Party, but popular support will not have been enhanced by Bristol South MP Dawn Primarolo refusing to pay her poll tax or by the de-selection by his ward Party of Bristol's first black mayor, Jim Williams.

Down in Cornwall the inspiration of the late David Penhaligon fires the Liberal Democrats. Distance from the political culture of the South East and a traditional independence make the current Conservative hold less tenacious than bare figures suggest. In Devon too, there are opportunities for Liberal progress: personal popularity will protect Emma Nicholson in Torridge & West Devon, but Nick Harvey is already running strongly in Devon North. In both Devon and Cornwall wages are amongst the lowest in the country, and the poll tax had a devastating effect in these two formerly low-rated counties.

Down on the south coast, Plymouth is dominated by the shadow of David Owen, still MP for Devonport, and at time of writing yet to announce whether he will stand again. The other two Plymouth seats are complicated by the demise of the ex-SDP vote and a Labour revival. The Tories have a 16.4% majority in Torbay, but with the Liberals ahead in local elections, an upset even here is an outside possibility. In Exeter a Labour revival led by John Lloyd is making the seat look like a three way marginal.

Back 'up country', Bath remains a Liberal Democrat target despite Christopher Patten's continuing hold on the helm of the Conservative leadership; the Liberals will also harbour ambitions for Weston-Super-Mare.

BATH

Con maj 1,412:

Con	23,515	45.4%
SDP	22,103	42.7%
Lab	5,507	10.6%
Grn	687	1.3%

Swing required 1.9%. **Category** Liberal Democrat target. **MP** Chris Patten **Lib Dem PPC** Nick Westbrook **Lab PPC** Pam Richards

Bath has all the potential to become a by-election type of contest: voters easily identify with the constituency they live in, and the local *Evening Chronicle* takes politics seriously.

Chris Patten is a very high-profile Conservative Chairman, relaxed on television and comfortably ensconced on the Party's 'social market' wing. Yet he has had his critics in Bath: local shopkeepers organised in BARRB (Businesses Against Rent/Rate Rises in Bath) have been up in arms over the Unified Business Rate which has led to shop closures in the city.

The SDP candidate in 1987, *Guardian* journalist Malcolm Dean, fought an up-beat campaign which squeezed the Labour vote. Yet Labour have recently revived – they did so well in the 1990 local elections that their constituency-wide newsletter was able to proclaim the banner headline 'Labour in the Lead'. Their candidate, Pam Richards, is a respected City Councillor.

Liberal Democrat Nick Westbrook, new to Bath but with a fortunate background in marketing, points out that Labour have often polled well here in local elections but have come third in parliamentary elections since 1966.

True to the by-election analogy, there is massive potential here for tactical voting – in a variety of ways. Potentially a fascinating contest.

BRISTOL EAST

Con maj 4,123:		
	Con 21,906	43.6%
	Lab 17,783	35.4%
	Lib 10,247	20.4%

Swing required 4.1%. **Category** Labour easier win. **MP** Jonathan Sayeed **Lab PPC** Jean Corston **Lib Dem PPC** John Kiely

Captured by Jonathan Sayeed from Tony Benn in 1983, this predominantly working-class constituency swung still further to the Tories in 1983 when Labour fielded the left-wing former MP for Bristol North West, Ron Thomas.

Former full-time Labour organiser and a proven tactician, Jean Corston is a model of Kinnockite orthodoxy on most issues, including electoral reform. Nevertheless, the Tories may seek to make political capital out of her refusal to pay the poll tax until served with a liability order.

John Kiely draws comfort from the Liberal Democrat vote in the 1990 local elections, slightly up on 1987 at a low point for the Party in the polls. Formerly a City Councillor for seven years in the inner-city ward of Easton, he insists that Labour have 'sold out the working people'.

Whilst Labour are the clear challenger here, a colourful campaign can be expected in this 'south of England style' seat which Labour must win to deprive the Conservatives of an overall majority.

BRISTOL NORTH WEST

Con maj 6,952:		
	Con 26,953	46.6%
	Lab 20,001	34.6%
	SDP 10,885	18.8%

Swing required 6%. **Category** Labour decider. **MP** Michael Stern **Lab PPC** Doug Naysmith **Lib Dem PPC** John Taylor

With the partial exception of February 1974, the party winning Bristol North West has won the general election overall. In 1987 the Conservative lead here was 12% compared with a lead of 11.5% in the country as a whole.

The seat is socially varied. It takes in large Council estates (Southmead in particular has many social problems) and the port of Avonmouth, as well as some strong Conservative areas. Both Rolls Royce and Aerospace are located in the constituency, at Filton. With redundancies in the air, defence is likely to be an issue; but unlike 1987, it is not so clear which Party this will favour.

Michael Stern has probably the lowest public profile of any Bristol MP. Liberal John Taylor will seek to draw attention to alleged City Council 'waste' – Bristol was due to set the third highest poll tax in the country (£524) for 1991/2. Mr Taylor lives on the fringe of Southmead and is not afraid to take the fight into Labour's heartland.

Doug Naysmith represents Hillfield ward on the Council and is Chair of the Docks Committee. As a supporter of PR and with a reputation as a 'moderate', he may be well placed to draw support from the centre ground.

BRISTOL WEST

Con maj 7,703:

Con	24,695	45.5%
Lib	16,992	31.3%
Lab	11,337	20.9%
Grn	1,096	2.0%
Oth	134	0.2%

Swing required 7.1%. **Category** Liberal Democrat target. **MP** William Waldegrave **Lib Dem PPC** Charles Boney

Bristol West covers the leafiest part of the city: Clifton, Henleaze and Stoke Bishop. It contains Bristol zoo and the headquarters of BBC South West.

Charles Boney sits on the City Council for Cabot ward, which includes Bristol University. As Bristol West has the sixth largest student population of any constituency in the country, Mr Boney intends to make education a big election issue.

William Waldegrave has risen steadily through government ranks into the cabinet, and is now Health Secretary. His aristocratic style and early comment that the NHS was 'not a market place' seem to suit local tastes.

Labour's local campaign has been short-circuited, temporarily at least, by internal wrangles over the archaic electoral college system used to select a PPC. Sources suggest the likely winner of the contest will be Jennie Smith, who fought Bath in 1987.

Charles Boney's only realistic hope in this seat is to squeeze the Labour vote and hope Mr Ashdown's post-Ribble surge continues. As Labour out-polled the Liberal

Democrats in the 1990 local elections, he will need to establish his credentials clearly as the effective challenger.

CORNWALL NORTH

Con maj 5,682:

Con 29,862	51.7%
Lib 24,180	41.9%
Lab 3,719	6.4%

Swing required 4.9%. **Category** Liberal Democrat target. **MP** Gerry Neale **Lib Dem PPC** Paul Tyler **Lab PPC** Frank Jordan

Cornwall North stretches from Newquay to just north of Bude. Inland it includes Bodmin, Launceston and a swathe of rural hinterland. Parliamentary elections in this beautiful part of Britain have followed a remarkably similar pattern since 1979 when Liberal John Pardoe lost the seat to solicitor Gerry Neale.

The local Liberal Democrats have around 900 members, and they distribute regular and professional-looking newsletters. There are plenty of local issues for Mr Tyler to get his teeth into. As elsewhere in Cornwall, the poll tax was particularly unpopular, hitting even the 'retirement vote', generally assumed to be pro-Tory. Small businesses have been hit hard by high interest rates and the UBR – sub post-offices and village shops are finding it difficult to survive. The future of the Longland Post-Natal Unit at Launceston is in question; and unemployment generally is high – around 20% in Newquay out of season.

Paul Tyler is a strong candidate. He has a long Cornish ancestory traced back to 1066. He has political experience going back to the 1960s as a County Councillor, MP for the old seat of Bodmin, and Chairman of the Liberal Party (1983-6); yet he has still not reached 50. He has worked in the media, for Shelter, and as a public affairs consultant specialising in environmental issues.

DEVON NORTH

Con maj 4,469:

Con 28,071	50.9%
Lib 23,602	42.8%
Lab 3,467	6.3%

Swing required 4.1%. **Category** Liberal Democrat target. **MP** Tony Spellar **Lib Dem PPC** Nick Harvey **Lab PPC** Paul Donnar

Devon North stretches along the coast from the prosperous market town of Barnstable through the depressed holiday resort of Ilfracombe to picturesque Lynton in the east. It contains a huge swathe of rural Devon, and over 10% of its population are employed in agriculture.

The constituency was represented from 1959 to 1979 by Jeremy Thorpe, former Liberal leader whose political career ended in controversy. He lost the seat to Tony Spellar, the current MP.

Since then, the Liberals have been gradually recovering their position, bucking the national trend with a 4% swing in 1987. Their PPC, Nick Harvey, is going about his task with gusto and some panache. He has labelled Mr Spellar the 'Great Abstainer': according to Mr Harvey, the MP has voted for the poll tax and NHS reforms and then 'wriggled with the wind when he realised there's local opposition'. Certainly the Conservatives have been forced on to the defensive over the proposal for the entire North Devon Health Authority to opt out.

The hardest battle for this seat may take place in the sleepy small towns and villages. As a parliamentary lobbyist by profession Nick Harvey is used to the corridors of Westminster, but he has been out getting his boots muddy campaigning to save village shops and schools: 'We do get up to some remote places, I've knocked on some doors where I'm sure they still haven't recovered from the shock of having a politician call'.

EXETER

Con maj 7,656:

Con	26,922	44.4%
SDP	19,266	31.8%
Lab	13,643	22.5%
Grn	597	1.0%
Oth	209	0.3%

Swing required 6.3%. **Category** Three way marginal. **MP** John Hannam **Lib Dem PPC** Graham Oakes **Lab PPC** John Lloyd

Devon's attractive county town on the Exe estuary was held for Labour by Gwynneth Dunwoody from 1966 to 1970. Since then it has been held by John Hannam (known in Parliament for his work on disabilities), although his share of the vote has declined since 1979. In 1987 the SDP's Mike Thomas ran a high-profile campaign to come second, but in the 1990 local elections Labour were in first place in the constituency.

Labour are fielding John Lloyd, a well-known local Councillor whose barrister's chambers are a stone's throw from the High Street. Liberal Democrat Graham Oakes, currently moving to Exeter from Yeovil, is a believer in the 'traditional Liberal approach, but with computers'.

Mr Lloyd and Mr Oakes have very similar politics. Oakes supports higher income tax to improve education and the NHS. Lloyd believes that 'people have a perception of Labour locally being sensible, good managers, people they know' – he is a supporter of PR and a written constitution.

Both opposition candidates insist they are running second to the Conservatives. Unless a clear challenger emerges, John Hannam could afford to drop more than a few votes and still hold Exeter.

FALMOUTH & CAMBOURNE

Con maj 5,039:

Con	23,725	43.9%
SDP	18,686	34.6%
Lab	11,271	20.9%

Swing required 4.7%. **Category** Liberal Democrat target. **MP** David Mudd (retiring), **Con PPC** Sebastian Coe **Lib Dem PPC** Terrye Jones **Lab PPC** John Cosgrove

David Mudd, former newspaper journalist and television presenter, has been an extremely popular local MP, partly because of his warmth and independence of mind, and partly because of his sheer commitment to the Cornish. In a part of the world where 'up country' can mean Devon rather than Bristol, Mr Mudd has been seen as the Falmouth man sticking up for his own. Sebastian Coe, therefore, is a strange choice of replacement, and fronting London's bid for the Olympic Games cuts little ice down here. Mr Coe 'wouldn't know his Burras from his Breage' (as they say).

Cornwall has a deep sense both that it is separate from England and that it has been badly treated by the Westminster Government. The recent ending of state support, and the consequent closure of the tin mine at South Crofty was roundly condemned – David Mudd led the last-minute deputations to the Government. High interest rates have punished local businesses working on tight profit margins, and the poll tax was deeply resented in a previously low-rated area.

The SDP candidate in 1987, barrister Jonathan Marks, achieved a 6.5% swing. Terrye Jones, Vice-Chairman of Kerrier Council, hopes to carry on where Mr Marks left off. Mrs Jones, who lives with her husband and children in Helston, was originally elected to the Council as an Independent and regards herself as 'an ordinary person who happened to get into politics'. In fact she isn't ordinary at all, but very warm, witty and highly articulate – with a born gift for 'soundbites'. She may well make Mr Coe seem like a little boy lost.

John Cosgrove, Cornish born-and-bred and a teacher in Falmouth with four children, is a thoughtful Christian socialist. He stood in 1987 and his campaign is already off to a flying start distributing newsletters making the point that David Mudd is the only Tory MP the constituency has ever had (his predecessors were Labour). Demography is against him in the sense that Falmouth is not as industrial as it was, but it is still far from the 'theme park' Cornwall of the picture postcard.

Media pundits get your maps out – Seb Coe is in trouble.

KINGSWOOD

Con maj 4,393:		
	Con 26,300	44.9%
	Lab 21,907	37.4%
	SDP 10,382	17.7%

Swing required 3.8%. **Category** Labour easier win. **MP** Robert Hayward **Lab PPC** Roger Berry **Lib Dem PPC** Jeanne Pinkerton

Divided between the City and Kingswood borough, this is nonetheless the most self-contained of the five Bristol seats. Many of the inhabitants are skilled workers employed at Rolls Royce and Aerospace, and defence was reputedly an issue in 1983 when Robert Hayward snatched the seat from Labour.

Mr Hayward is a popular local MP. In his own words he 'lives, shops and worships in the constituency', and he also referees rugby matches. He is well-known in the House of Commons as an amateur psephologist, and was consulted by several cabinet ministers as the most perceptive student of MPs' voting intentions in the November 1991 Conservative leadership election.

Roger Berry, Labour leader on Avon County Council and an economics lecturer at Bristol University, is an articulate and capable opponent. Liberal Democrat Jeanne Pinkerton runs a local newsagents where Hayward has been known to pop in for a paper. Ms Pinkerton is an experienced campaigner and well aware that both Mr Hayward and Mr Berry have the 'moderate' credentials to poach the centre ground.

There are plenty of local issues. Robert Hayward and Roger Berry were agreed in opposing the siting of the Bristol Rovers ground in Mangotsfield; they differ over the proposal for a Kingswood Technology College, as Berry regards the MP's support for the plan as 'straight populism'.

Kingswood is technically the most marginal of the Conservative-held Bristol seats and one Labour must be very hopeful of capturing. But Robert Hayward commands a personal vote and will not be easily removed.

PLYMOUTH DRAKE

Con maj 3,125:		
	Con 16,195	41.3%
	SDP 13,070	33.3%
	Lab 9,451	24.1%
	Grn 493	1.3%

Swing required 4% to Liberal Democrats, 8.6% to Labour. **Category** Three way marginal. **MP** Dame Janet Fookes **Lib Dem PPC** Valerie Cox **Lab PPC** Peter Telford

Peter Telford, dubbed 'the most eligible bachelor in the South West' by *Company* magazine, has disappointed female admirers by announcing his engagement. Nonetheless, Labour has showed well in local government elections and will conduct a vigorous campaign.

Cornwall-based Valerie Cox was selected as late as January 1991 and has little time to establish her claim to take over where the SDP's David Astor left off in 1987. Plymouth Drake borders Plymouth Devonport, currently held by Dr David Owen. With the probable decline of the 'Owen factor', former SDP-voters are the unknown factor in this electoral equation.

This could be a very interesting contest if a by-election mentality develops. However, the constituency is not a natural community - more the central slice of the city designed by the Boundary Commission in the early 1980s and named after the man who gave us potatoes and tobacco. In the face of a divided opposition, Dame Janet Fookes could hold on with less than 40% of the vote.

PLYMOUTH SUTTON

Con maj 4,123:

Con 23,187 45.8%

Lib 19,174 37.8%

Lab 8,310 16.4%

Swing required 4%. **Category** Liberal Democrat target. **MP** Alan Clark **Lib Dem PPC** Julian Brett-Freeman **Lab PPC** Andrew Pawley

Consisting mainly of Plympton and Plymstock, Sutton is the most middle-class of the Plymouth constituencies, with a large number of elderly people and commuters.

Newcomer Julian Brett-Freeman is more used to the politics of Tower Hamlets than of Devon, and is acutely aware of the need to squeeze the Labour vote. He will need to convince Labour voters to vote tactically, retain the 'Owenite' vote and benefit from an improved national Liberal Democrat showing.

However, old Etonian Alan Clark, currently the Minister for Defence procurement, is regarded as something of a maverick, and an upset cannot be entirely ruled out.

ST IVES

Con maj 7,555:

Con 25,174 48.3%

SDP 17,619 33.8%

Lab 9,275 17.8%

Swing required 7.8%. **Category** Liberal Democrat target. **MP** David Harris **Lib Dem PPC** Andrew George **Lab PPC** Steve Warren

St Ives is the most westerly constituency in Britain, including the Scilly Isles, Lands End, Penzance, Helston and St Ives itself. Tourism is very important to the local economy, particularly along the granite coastline. Penzance is the largest town with a population of around 20,000. The local MP has been Conservative since 1945, David Harris replacing former Defence Secretary John Nott, who stood down in 1983.

Liberal Democrat Andrew George, born at Mullion in the constituency, is a field worker for the Rural Community Council and co-author of *Cornwall at the Crossroads*. He will put balanced economic development, homes for local people and the environment at the heart of his campaign.

Labour PPC Steve Warren is a leading member of a well organised Labour Group on Penwith District Council and, as Chair of the Housing Committee, has a high local profile.

The question of sewage disposal has been a major local issue. The present system of discharging raw sewage into Mounts Bay on the south coast and St Ives Bay in the north has long been regarded as less than ideal. In response to public pressure, South West Water originally proposed pumping raw sewage to a deep sea outlet off Gwithian in the north, but have now agreed to an expensive scheme to pump all sewage to Hayle for primary and secondary treatment.

Tin mine closures, the current recession, and environmental issues have been given extensive coverage in local newspapers and may have undermined Conservative credibility in Cornwall. St Ives is clearly something of a long shot for the Liberal Democrats, but Mr Harris will not regard his seat as entirely safe.

WESTON-SUPER-MARE

Con maj 7,998:		
	Con 28,547	49.4%
	SDP 20,549	35.6%
	Lab 6,584	11.4%
	Grn 2,067	3.6%

Swing required 7.9%. **Category** Liberal Democrat target. **MP** Jerry Wiggin **Lib Dem PPC** Brian Cotter **Lab PPC** David Murray

The town of Weston-Super-Mare is situated beside miles of mud-flats on the Avon side of the Severn estuary. The Severn contains a wide variety of pollutants: Greenpeace reported in 1987 that zinc concentration is 30 times greater than in the open North Atlantic. What is more, Hinkley B nuclear power station has had several emergency shut-downs.

All this may account for the relatively good showing for the Greens in 1987. The Conservative vote has slipped consistently since 1979, but Labour did not recover in 1987 the ground they had lost in 1983. So there seems to be some opportunity for

Brian Cotter to advance if he can seize the environmental mantle. Jerry Wiggin is unashamedly on the right of the Conservative Party, which may help his leading challenger.

WALES

In 1987 there was a 4.5% swing in Wales from the Conservatives to Labour, who captured four seats. The Alliance and Plaid Cymru captured one each. With the addition of the by-election gain in the Vale of Glamorgan, Labour now holds 25 seats in Wales, the Tories seven, the Liberal Democrats three and Plaid Cymru three.

There are no signs that Peter Walker's efforts as Welsh Secretary will be translated into a Tory recovery. Other seats are now within Labour's range – Cardiff Central, Delyn, and Pembroke. Conwy is a possibility for the Liberal Democrats as well as Labour. Labour would need a 9.3% swing to capture Cardiff North, which is an outside possibility.

Whatever its appeal elsewhere, the strident tones of 1980s Conservatism has found few echoes in Wales, and the dwindling band of Conservative MPs are likely to be even fewer in number, and more beleaguered, after the general election. This will almost certainly strengthen the desire for the devolution of political power to Wales from London, whatever the overall result.

CARDIFF CENTRAL

Con maj 1,986:		
	Con 15,241	37.1%
	Lab 13,255	32.3%
	Lib 12,062	29.4%
	PC 535	1.3%

Swing required 2.4%. **Category** Labour easier win. **MP** Ian Grist **Lab PPC** Jon Jones **Lib Dem PPC** Jenny Randerson

The poll tax was enormously unpopular in south Wales and has led to ever-greater disillusionment with the Westminster Government. Ian Grist, a Cardiff MP since February 1974, was removed from his post as Under-Secretary for Wales in Mr Major's first reshuffle, allegedly because of his support for Mr Heseltine in the Conservative leadership contest.

The replacement for the distinctly 'wet' Grist was the distinctly 'dry' Nicholas

Bennett, the MP for Pembroke, whose accession to government office was followed shortly by the scrapping of the tax. Ironically perhaps, it is therefore Ian Grist who may be seen as the man who gave Cardiff the poll tax.

Ready to take advantage of Mr Grist's discomfort is Jon Jones, biology teacher and City Councillor, but he will need to demonstrate quickly and clearly that he is the main challenger.

CONWY

Con maj 3,730:

Con	15,730	38.7%
Lib	12,706	31.2%
Lab	9,049	22.3%
PC	3,177	7.8%

Swing required 3.8% for Liberal Democrats, 8.2% for Labour. **Category** Three way marginal. **MP** Sir Wyn Roberts **Lib Dem PPC** Roger Roberts **Lab PPC** Betty Williams **PC PPC** Rhodri Davies

The bulk of the population in this north Wales constituency live in towns by the sea. Llandudno is an elegant and charming resort which first flourished in the Victorian age, and has now a growing elderly population and consequent 'retirement vote'. Bangor, by contrast, with its university, has a large young vote. Conwy itself is mainly renowned for its imposing castle, built by Edward I as part of his subjugation of the unruly Welsh.

Times have changed since the thirteenth century, and this is now a sedate rather than unruly corner of the world. Its inclination is conservative and its MP, since 1970, is Conservative – Sir Wyn Roberts, formerly a broadcaster with Harlech television. Set to contest the seat for the third time is Sir Wyn's namesake, the methodist minister and dynamic campaigner Roger Roberts.

Entering the field for the second time is Gwynedd County Councillor Betty Williams, who increased Labour's share of the vote in 1987 by over 5%. The 'North West factor' has not yet, however, reached this far into north Wales and a tussle between 'Roberts the telly' and 'Roberts the pulpit' seems the more likely bet.

DELYN

Con maj 1,224:

Con	21,728	41.4%
Lab	20,504	39.1%
Lib	8,913	17.0%
PC	1,339	2.5%

Swing required 1.7%. **Category** Labour easier win. **MP** Keith Raffan (retiring) **Con PPC** Michael Whitby **Lab PPC** David Hanson

Delyn is geographically and culturally close to Merseyside and the North West of England, which may partly explain the 5% swing to Labour in 1987. The Conservative majority now looks precarious, and Labour will be encouraged by the late selection of a PPC (March 1991) – Michael Whitby was preferred to Tony Sharps, the Leader of Delyn Council, who promptly resigned from the Party.

The seat is socially balanced. Flint, its largest town, is very industrial and inclines to Labour. Prestatyn has a large 'retirement vote' and inclines to the Conservatives.

Labour PPC David Hanson, a 34 year-old charity official, hails from Northwich but is on the brink of moving to Delyn. This surely indicates his optimism.

MONMOUTH

Con maj 9,950:

Con	22,387	47.5%
Lab	13,037	27.7%
SDP	11,313	24.0%
PC	363	0.8%

Swing required 9.9% for Labour, 11.8% for Liberal Democrats. **Category** Three way marginal. **MP** vacant **Con PPC** Roger Evans **Lab PPC** Huw Edwards **Lib Dem PPC** Frances David

Following the death of Sir John Stradling Thomas, a by-election is pending in Monmouth as this book goes to press. It appears a no-win situation for the Government: by-elections these days are made for protest. What remains unclear at this time is whether one of the opposition parties can draw clear of the other during the campaign and thus attract the anti-government vote. In other words, is this a Mid Staffs or a Ribble Valley?

PEMBROKE

Con maj 5,700:

Con	23,314	41.0%
Lab	17,614	31.0%
Lib	14,832	26.1%
PC	1,119	2.0%

Swing required 5%. **Category** Labour decider. **MP** Nicholas Bennett **Lab PPC** Nick Ainger **Lib Dem PPC** Aza Pinney **PC PPC** Conrad Bryant

Pembroke is situated at the westerly tip of Wales taking in the industrial port of Milford Haven, Fishguard (whence the ferry leaves for Ireland), and the 'English' area around Haverford West. The hinterland is pleasantly rural.

Nicholas Edwards, the local Conservative MP from 1970 to 1987 was generally considered to be a 'wet', but this did not stop him from sitting in Mrs Thatcher's cabinet as Secretary of State for Wales from 1979 until his retirement from the House of Commons.

His successor, Nicholas Bennett is more of a 'dry'. In John Major's first reshuffle he bcame Under Secretary for Wales, replacing Ian Grist, Cardiff Central MP, who had supported Michael Heseltine's leadership bid.

Nick Ainger, a County Councillor, was born and bred locally, is personable and has a good public profile. He will need to appeal to the centre ground in a seat that was represented after the War by Lloyd George's son and where the Liberals gained 6% in 1987 on the 1983 SDP showing.

Conservative Central Office will be keen to hold their western outpost in Wales, and Nicholas Bennett will hope that the opposition to him continues to be divided.

VALE OF GLAMORGAN

Con maj 6,251:

Con	24,229	46.8%
Lab	17,978	34.7%
SDP	8,633	16.7%
PC	946	1.8%

Swing required 6.1%. **Category** Labour decider. **MP** John Smith (Labour) **Con PPC** Walter Sweeny **Lib Dem PPC** Andrew Toye **PC PPC** David Hastwell

Following the death in 1989 of Sir Raymond Gower, the Vale's MP for 38 years, Labour won by 6,000 votes a by-election campaign that was short on policy but long on the 'plain common sense' of its candidate John Smith.

Mr Smith has developed a reputation as a conscientious constituency MP. The Vale has a varied population – Barry is industrial but inland is rural with many villages on the way up to Pontypridd.

Famous by-election victors have often come a cropper in the subsequent next general election. If Labour are within breathing distance of the Conservatives in the national polls, John Smith will probably hold on.

Index to Profiles

Amber Valley, 81
Ayr, 117

Barrow & Furness, 102
Basildon, 125
Bath, 141
Batley & Spen, 94
Battersea, 66
Birmingham Hall Green, 81
Birmingham Northfield, 82
Birmingham Selly Oak, 82
Birmingham Yardley, 83
Blackpool North, 102
Blackpool South, 103
Bolton North East, 103
Bolton West, 104
Brentford & Isleworth, 67
Bristol East, 142
Bristol North West, 142
Bristol West, 143
Burton, 83
Bury North, 104
Bury South, 105

Calder Valley, 94
Cambridge, 125
Cambridgeshire North East, 126
Cannock & Burntwood, 83
Cardiff Central, 150
Chelmsford, 126
Cheltenham, 127
Chester, 105
Chorley, 106
Colne Valley, 95
Congleton, 106
Conwy, 151
Corby, 127

Cornwall North, 144
Coventry South West, 84
Crosby, 107
Croydon North West, 68

Darlington, 95
Davyhulme, 107
Delyn, 151
Derby North, 85
Derbyshire South, 85
Devon North, 144
Dover, 128
Dudley West, 86
Dulwich, 68
Dumfries, 118

Eastbourne, 129
Eastwood, 118
Edinburgh Pentlands, 119
Edinburgh West, 120
Edmonton, 69
Ellesmere Port & Neston, 108
Elmet, 96
Eltham, 69
Erewash, 86
Erith & Crayford, 70
Exeter, 145

Falmouth & Cambourne, 146
Feltham & Heston, 71
Fulham, 71

Galloway & Upper Nithsdale, 120
Gravesham, 129

Hampstead & Highgate, 72
Harlow, 130

index

Hayes & Harlington, 73
Hazel Grove, 108
Hereford, 87
High Peak, 109
Hornsey & Wood Green, 73
Hyndburn, 110

Ilford South, 74
Ipswich, 130
Isle of Wight, 131

Keighley, 96
Kensington, 74
Kincardine & Deeside, 121
Kingswood, 147

Lancashire West, 110
Lancaster, 111
Langbaurgh, 97
Leeds North West, 97
Leicestershire North West, 87
Lewisham East, 75
Lewisham West, 75
Lincoln, 88
Littleborough & Saddleworth, 111
Luton South, 131

Milton Keynes South West, 132
Mitcham & Morden, 76
Monmouth, 152

North East Milton Keynes, 133
Northampton North, 133
Norwich North, 134
Nottingham East, 88
Nottingham South, 89
Nuneaton, 90

Oxford West & Abingdon, 135

Pembroke, 152
Pendle, 112
Perth & Kinross, 122

Peterborough, 135
Plymouth Drake, 147
Plymouth Sutton, 148
Portsmouth South, 136
Pudsey, 98
Putney, 76

Ribble Valley, 113
Richmond & Barnes, 77
Rossendale & Darwen, 113

Sheffield Hallam, 98
Sherwood, 90
Slough, 136
South Ribble, 114
Southampton Itchen, 137
Southampton Test, 137
St Ives, 148
Staffordshire Mid, 91
Stevenage, 138
Stirling, 122
Stockport, 114
Stockton South, 99
Streatham, 78
Swindon, 139

Tayside North, 123
Thurrock, 139
Tynemouth, 99

Vale of Glamorgan, 153

Wallasey, 114
Walthamstow, 78
Warrington South, 115
Warwickshire North, 91
Westminster North, 79
Weston-Super-Mare, 149
Wolverhampton North East, 92
Wyre Forest, 92

York, 100

Notes on Contributors

Nina Fishman is Senior Lecturer in Politics and History, Harrow College, Polytechnic of Central London.

Peter Hanington is a freelance journalist.

Tim Johnson is a publisher in information technology.

Charles Kennedy is President of the Liberal Democrats, and Member of Parliament for Ross, Cromarty and Skye.

David Marquand is Professor of Politics, University of Sheffield.

Austin Mitchell is the Labour Member of Parliament for Great Grimsby, and a televison journalist.

Stephen Robinson is Political Researcher for Common Voice.

Gareth Smyth is Press and Broadcasting Officer for Common Voice.

Seth Weir is a freelance researcher/journalist.

Stuart Weir has been editor of *New Socialist* and is associate editor of *New Statesman & Society*.

About Common Voice

Operating from a centre-left perspective Common Voice exists to encourage debate and discussion across the political spectrum.

Common Voice has published:
The Intelligent Person's Guide to Electoral Reform, by Helena Catt
Co-operation and Conflict: Politics in the Hung Counties, by Steve Leach and Chris Game.

Common Voice can be contacted at Garden Studios, 11-15 Betterton Street, London WC2H 9BP Tel: 071-379 0344 Fax: 071-379 0801.